Fidel Castro

These and other titles are included in The Importance Of biography series:

Maya Angelou	Harry Houdini
Louis Armstrong	Thomas Jefferson
James Baldwin	Mother Jones
Lucille Ball	John F. Kennedy
The Beatles	Martin Luther King Jr.
Alexander Graham Bell	Bruce Lee
Napoleon Bonaparte	John Lennon
Julius Caesar	Abraham Lincoln
Rachel Carson	Joe Louis
Charlie Chaplin	Douglas MacArthur
Charlemagne	Thurgood Marshall
Winston Churchill	Margaret Mead
Christopher Columbus	Golda Meir
Leonardo da Vinci	Mother Teresa
James Dean	Muhammad
Charles Dickens	John Muir
Walt Disney	Richard M. Nixon
Dr. Seuss	Pablo Picasso
F. Scott Fitzgerald	Edgar Allan Poe
Anne Frank	Elvis Presley
Benjamin Franklin	Queen Elizabeth I
Mohandas Gandhi	Franklin D. Roosevelt
John Glenn	Queen Victoria
Jane Goodall	Jonas Salk
Martha Graham	Margaret Sanger
Lorraine Hansberry	William Shakespeare
Stephen Hawking	Frank Sinatra
Ernest Hemingway	Tecumseh
Adolf Hitler	Simon Wiesenthal

THE IMPORTANCE OF

Fidel Castro

by Adam Woog

LUCENT
BOOKS®

THOMSON

™

GALE

San Diego • Detroit • New York • San Francisco • Cleveland • New Haven, Conn. • Waterville, Maine • London • Munich

THOMSON
——✦——™
GALE

To my grandmother, Ruby Barham.

LIBRARY OF CONGRESS CATALOGING-IN-PUBLICATION DATA

Woog, Adam, 1953–.
  Fidel Castro / Adam Woog.
    p. cm. — (The importance of)
Includes bibliographical references and index.
  Summary: Profiles the life of the Cuban leader, including his upbringing, his
education, his political influences, his role in the Cuban revolution, and his government
of the island nation.
  ISBN 1-59018-231-6 (hardback : alk. paper)
  1. Castro, Fidel, 1927– —Juvenile literature. 2. Cuba—History—1933–1959—
Juvenile literature. 3. Cuba—History—1959– —Juvenile literature. 4. Heads of
state—Cuba—Biography—Juvenile literature. 5. Revolutionaries—Cuba—Biography—
Juvenile literature. I. Title. II. Series.
  F1788.22.C3W66 2003
  972.9106'4'092—dc21
                                                                        2002014363

Printed in the United States of America

Contents

Foreword

THE IMPORTANCE OF biography series deals with individuals who have made a unique contribution to history. The editors of the series have deliberately chosen to cast a wide net and include people from all fields of endeavor. Individuals from politics, music, art, literature, philosophy, science, sports, and religion are all represented. In addition, the editors did not restrict the series to individuals whose accomplishments have helped change the course of history. Of necessity, this criterion would have eliminated many whose contribution was great, though limited. Charles Darwin, for example, was responsible for radically altering the scientific view of the natural history of the world. His achievements continue to impact the study of science today. Others, such as Chief Joseph of the Nez Percé, played a pivotal role in the history of their own people. While Joseph's influence does not extend much beyond the Nez Percé, his nonviolent resistance to white expansion and his continuing role in protecting his tribe and his homeland remain an inspiration to all.

These biographies are more than factual chronicles. Each volume attempts to emphasize an individual's contributions both in his or her own time and for posterity. For example, the voyages of Christopher Columbus opened the way to European colonization of the New World. Unquestionably, his encounter with the New World brought monumental changes to both Europe and the Americas in his day. Today, however, the broader impact of Columbus's voyages is being critically scrutinized. *Christopher Columbus,* as well as every biography in The Importance Of series, includes and evaluates the most recent scholarship available on each subject.

Each author includes a wide variety of primary and secondary source quotations to document and substantiate his or her work. All quotes are footnoted to show readers exactly how and where biographers derive their information, as well as provide stepping-stones to further research. These quotations enliven the text by giving readers eyewitness views of the life and times of each individual covered in The Importance Of series.

Finally, each volume is enhanced by photographs, bibliographies, chronologies, and comprehensive indexes. For both the casual reader and the student engaged in research, The Importance Of biographies will be a fascinating adventure into the lives of people who have helped shape humanity's past and present, and who will continue to shape its future.

Important Dates in the Life of Fidel Castro

1958
The guerrilla war by Castro's forces succeeds in critically weakening the Batista regime.

1960
Castro signs a major trade agreement with the Soviet Union; The United States begins a partial economic embargo against Cuba because of Castro's anti-American stance.

August 13, 1926
Fidel Alejandro Castro Ruz is born in Birán, Oriente Province, Cuba.

1955
Batista grants amnesty to Castro; Castro goes into exile in Mexico to plot a Cuban invasion and meets Ernesto "Che" Guevara.

1950
Castro begins to practice law in Havana and joins the reform Ortodoxos Party.

1945
Castro enters the University of Havana Law School.

1944
Castro is named the best high-school athlete in Cuba.

1962
The United States imposes a full-trade embargo on Cuba; Cuban missile crisis nearly causes war between the United States and Soviet Union.

1925

1945

1965

1947
Castro joins an unsuccessful attempt to invade the Dominican Republic.

1948
Castro marries Mirta Díaz-Balart; Participates in urban riots in Bogotá, Colombia.

1952
Castro begins to organize a secret revolutionary army.

July 26, 1953
Castro launches an armed struggle against dictator Fulgencio Batista; The attack on Moncada Barracks fails and Castro is sentenced to fifteen years in prison.

1956
Castro and his rebel soldiers sail to Cuba, but Batista's army kills or captures most of them and forces the survivors to hide in the Sierra Maestra Mountains.

1959
Batista flees; Castro makes triumphant journey to Havana and takes power.

1963
U.S. economic and social restrictions on Cuba are tightened further; Travel to the island by U.S. citizens is banned, as are all financial and commercial transactions.

1961
Washington breaks off diplomatic relations with Cuba; Central Intelligence Agency–backed, anti-Castro Cuban exiles are defeated during the Bay of Pigs invasion; Castro declares Cuba a socialist state.

1975
Castro sends troops to Angola to support a revolutionary army.

1977–1978
Castro sends troops to Ethiopia to help prevent invasion by Somalia; He also provides support to the Sandinista National Liberation Front in Nicaragua.

1979
Castro is elected chair of the Non-Aligned Movement. He serves in the position until 1982; Sends troops to Afghanistan to help the Soviets.

1980
The Mariel boatlift creates a mass exodus of 120,000 Cuban refugees to the United States.

1981
Following the inauguration of Ronald Reagan as president, the United States tightens its embargo on Cuba.

1998
Pope John Paul II visits Cuba; He condemns the U.S. trade embargo and calls for greater freedoms and personal responsibility on the island.

2001
Castro is nominated for the 2001 Nobel Peace Prize for his work with other developing nations; The first shipments of food from the United States to Cuba in almost forty years are allowed as a humanitarian gesture following a devastating hurricane.

1970   **1985**   **2000**

1977
Limited economic and cultural ties between Cuba and the United States resume, including a drop on the ban on travel to Cuba by U.S. citizens.

1967
Guevara, the second most important man in the Cuban revolution, is killed in Bolivia.

1982
The ban on travel to Cuba by U.S. citizens is reinstated.

1991
The collapse of the Soviet Union deals the Cuban economy a serious blow.

1992
U.S. president George H.W. Bush passes legislation effectively preventing the importation into Cuba of all food and medicine from any U.S. sources.

1994
Tens of thousands more Cubans flee on flimsy boats and rafts after Castro declares an open migration policy.

2002
Former president Jimmy Carter becomes the first sitting or former president to visit Cuba since the revolution.

1996
The Helms-Burton Act, tightening trade restrictions still further on Cuba, is signed into law by President Bill Clinton.

El Jefe

For over forty years, Fidel Castro has been *El Jefe,* the absolute leader of Cuba. He has dominated Cuban politics and society since 1959 with an intense, paternal strength, and his life is intimately woven into Cuba's history.

That year, Castro led an unlikely band of revolutionary soldiers to triumph over a corrupt and foreign-dominated government. As the new leader, he then radically transformed Cuba to conform with his deep commitment to socialist principles. Castro also became a major force in revolutionary movements around the world and an important figure in global politics.

Despite many attempts (both secret and open) to depose him, *El Jefe* has remained in power and held stubbornly to his beliefs. He has outlasted many friends, including the heads of several Communist countries, and enemies, including a succession of American presidents. Next to England's Queen Elizabeth II, Castro is the world's longest-serving head of state.

PASSION, PRO AND CON

Castro arouses strong feelings, both pro and con. Journalist Jon Lee Anderson writes, "Few leaders of the twentieth century have aroused such a widespread and enduring fascination as Cuba's Fidel Castro; rarely in modern times has a political event provoked such distinct passions as the revolution he led to power in 1959."[1]

For people all over the world, Castro was the quintessential hero—a defiant, imaginative, bold, and brilliantly unpredictable leader who restored Cuba's pride and independence after years of humiliating oppression. Although Castro has consistently insisted he is leading the country to a glorious future, many observers, including a large number of Cubans, have found his performance discouraging.

To his critics, Castro is ruthless and cunning, a tyrant who seized power and kept it, then failed to make good on his promises of fair treatment for all. They say he destroyed democracy in Cuba, silenced his critics, and antagonized other world leaders.

Furthermore, they blame Castro's policies for the country's ongoing economic woes. While acknowledging that the decades-long U.S. trade embargo against Cuba has done much to bring Cuba's economy to a near-ruinous state, his critics point out that Castro's implacable anti-

American stance has made lifting that embargo unlikely or prohibitively difficult for a series of presidents of both U.S. parties.

The truth about Castro may be somewhere in the middle, combining elements of the positive and negative. This muddiness—some good, some bad—is perhaps reflected in the simple fact that Castro has stayed in power so long. Even as he has overseen failed programs that have severely burdened the Cuban people, he has remained popular with millions of them. Castro is thus a living paradox: an extremely popular revolutionary who be-

Fidel Castro has governed Cuba since 1959 in a way some characterize as revolutionary and others as tyrannical.

came a dictator over the very people he vowed to liberate.

A CHARISMATIC LEADER

The man who arouses such passion is intensely charismatic. Castro has developed an instantly recognizable personal style. It is built around his physically imposing build, luxurious beard, ever-present cigar (until he gave up smoking in the 1980s during a national antismoking campaign), and unchanging wardrobe (at first combat fatigues, more recently a formal military uniform).

This visual style combines with a mesmerizing ability to inspire loyalty and convince others of his ideas through speaking. Castro has always been a brilliant speaker, with a gift for capturing and holding attention.

He is intensely physical, making liberal use of his voice, eyes, brows, hands, and body to make his point. He also has an astonishing memory and can easily speak for hours at a time. (His record is about nine hours, nonstop.) Furthermore, Castro can lecture authoritatively on a wide range of subjects, not just politics. Biographer Tad Szulc comments, "[H]e has opinions about everything from medicine to *haute cuisine.*"[2]

A point of pride with Castro is his habit of never preparing notes, even for marathon speeches. He prefers to improvise after reading the desires of his audience. Castro once remarked, "Often my speeches are conversations, exchanges of impressions with the public. . . . It is much like a conversation; and really when you are going to have a talk with somebody, you cannot plan the whole conversation."[3]

NOT A FREE CUBA

When Castro used his charisma to fuel his rise to power, it was an opportune moment. The revolution caught fire because Cubans were ready for a leader who promised a free and independent land. When Castro seized power, most Cubans were eager to follow him.

The desire for a free Cuba had been building for hundreds of years. For all that time, the island had been a colony of—or strongly influenced by—foreign countries.

For four hundred years after Christopher Columbus claimed it for Spain on his first voyage in 1492, Cuba, the largest island in the Caribbean, was a Spanish colony. The Spaniards exploited Cuba for its cattle, tobacco, sugarcane, and other crops.

Revolutionary struggles to free Cuba became intense in the late 1800s, and after decades of open rebellion the Spanish

A HEADY EXPERIENCE

Historian Hugh Thomas, in this passage from his book Cuba, or, The Pursuit of Freedom, *reflects on Castro's ability to persuade and direct Cuba for decades. Although Thomas updated his classic study in 1998, the following passage describes his outlook at the time of the first edition in 1971.*

Castro's magnetism and oratory have enabled him to direct Cuban society since 1959 very much according to his own designs. He has successfully persuaded many people that the absence of goods in the shops is a sign of virtue, that the market economy such as exists even in East Europe is an evil, that cities are vicious and that the countryside is noble. . . . [S]imilarly, in the past there were eloquent slave owners able to explain why there should be a Sunday only every ten days, and yet still be loved.

Further, Castro has done many things which have been popular even if they have been unjust to minorities or even if they have been at least partly designed to achieve popularity. Revolutionary Cuba has throughout enjoyed a quite new national spirit deriving from the heady experience of social revolution and international adventure. Castro's own personality, undoubtedly fortunate, apparently heroic, certainly indefatigable and formidable, is itself a phenomenon in which many Cubans can take pride.

"MAKING MAN BETTER"

In this excerpt from Lee Lockwood's book Castro's Cuba, Cuba's Fidel, *published in the first decade of Castro's rule,* El Jefe *is quoted on his feelings about serving mankind:*

As a Revolutionary, it is my understanding that one of our fundamental concerns must be that all the manifestations of culture be placed at the service of man, developing in him all the most positive feelings. For me, art is not an end in itself. Man is its end; making man happier, making man better. . . .

I don't think there has ever existed a society in which all the manifestations of culture have not been at the service of some cause or concept. Our duty is to see that the whole is at the service of the kind of man we wish to create.

were ousted in 1898. The United States played a large role in this, as part of the Spanish-American War. Americans generally saw their part in this affair as a good deed resulting in the liberation of some neighbors. However, for many Cubans the old masters were simply replaced with new ones.

Cuba became a free country in name, but in reality it was simply an annex of American business interests. American companies took over virtually all of the country's utilities and agriculture, including railways, banking, public utilities, fruit orchards, and sugarcane production.

A succession of corrupt, greedy, and pro-American dictators held sway. Only politicians who were sympathetic to American business interests reached levels of power. The constitutional rights of Cubans were ignored or twisted, its press censored, and its dissident voices terrorized by secret police and death squads. Unemployment and poverty were rampant. This was the world in which Fidel Castro grew up.

1 Young Fidel

Fidel Castro was born in what was then Cuba's Oriente Province. (The provincial borders have since changed, and the region has a different name.)

Oriente was in the southeast part of the island. Far from Havana, the nation's capital, it was isolated from government influence. The people who lived there were rugged farmers who were used to being on their own. Not surprisingly, they had a reputation as stubborn individualists who questioned government and resisted authority.

The province was also one of the poorest regions of the country. Unemployment sometimes ran as high as 50 percent. Most of the houses were little better than crude shacks, lacking even basic comforts such as running water. Medical help, education, and general hygiene were, at best, primitive.

Like most of Cuba, Oriente was completely dependent on agriculture, primarily sugar production. The region's huge sugarcane farms were primarily under the control of absentee landlords—that is, owners who did not live on the farms but controlled them from far away. Most of these absentee landlords were large, American-owned businesses or wealthy

Cubans, most of whom had emigrated from Spain or were the privileged children of Spanish settlers.

The people who actually worked in Oriente's sugarcane fields were far from being privileged. They were mostly illiterate, desperately poor peasants. Many were immigrants from Haiti of African ancestry, while the majority of the other residents were of mixed African and Spanish ancestry.

CASTRO'S FATHER

The Castro family was not an impoverished group of field workers; they were, in fact, wealthy landowners. Fidel's father, Ángel Castro Argiz, was one of the most powerful men in Oriente. He controlled an estate of about twenty-three thousand acres, called Las Manacas. According to some sources, Ángel also owned most of the buildings in the nearby village of Birán.

Although he was rich, Ángel was not an aristocrat. He had come to Cuba as an impoverished, teenaged orphan from the Spanish province of Galicia. He was an ambitious and hard worker, and by the age of thirty-five owned his own sugarcane farm. As time went on, Ángel steadily acquired more land.

Ángel never identified himself with other rich landowners. He rarely spent time with them, even after he had become one. Tough, unsophisticated, and nearly illiterate, he always felt more comfortable with the peasants he hired to work his land.

He took pride in personally helping to prepare and take breakfast to his workers every morning. Ángel also had a reputation for helping the people of the region when they were in particular need. Years later, his son Fidel remarked, "I can't recall his ever failing to find a solution whenever somebody asked him for something. Sometimes he grumbled and complained, but his generosity always got the upper hand."[4]

THE FAMILY GROWS

Despite his generous side, Ángel was also known for being the strict, absolute ruler of his dominion. Writer Robert E. Quirk notes, "He was a harsh taskmaster, much feared by the Jamaican and Cuban blacks who worked for him."[5]

Ángel was the master of the farmhouse where he and his family lived as well. This house was not a fine mansion, however, like those of Cuba's other wealthy farming families. Built of wood on stilts, in the style of its owner's native Galicia, it was more like a rough military barrack.

The large and boisterous Castro family jostled for space in the main section of the house. Cattle, chickens, and other livestock lived underneath it, in the area created by the stilts. The smell of livestock was a pungent and permanent feature of the house.

Ángel's first wife was a schoolteacher. She had two children who survived into adulthood: Pedro Emilio and Lidia. Then Ángel began an intense affair with Lina Ruz González, a young maid and cook in his household.

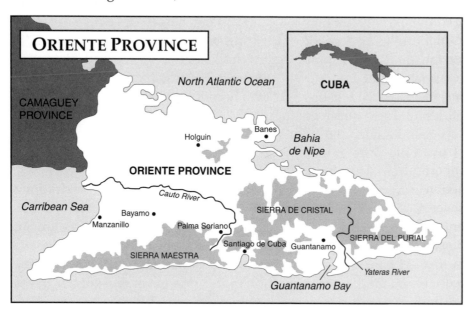

ORIENTE PROVINCE

North Atlantic Ocean

CUBA

CAMAGUEY PROVINCE

Holguin

Banes

Bahia de Nipe

ORIENTE PROVINCE

Carribean Sea

Cauto River

Bayamo

Manzanillo

Palma Soriano

SIERRA DE CRISTAL

SIERRA DEL PURIAL

Santiago de Cuba

Guantanamo

SIERRA MAESTRA

Yateras River

Guantanamo Bay

Castro converses with his mother Lina (right) before leaving Havana to attend the 1960 United Nations session. The Cuban leader has always admired his mother's strength.

As this affair deepened and became public knowledge, Ángel's wife left him. Because their Catholic religion forbade divorce, however, Lina and Ángel could not marry until his first wife died.

In the meantime, the two lived together and had more children. Three survived into adulthood: Ángela, Ramón, and Fidel. After Ángel and Lina were able to marry, four more children were born: Raúl, Juana, Emma, and Agustina.

Fidel remembers Lina, his mother, as talkative, friendly, forthright, and demonstrative—quite the opposite of his gruff and short-tempered father. He also recalls her as a tough-minded woman who worked hard to maintain her large and demanding household, at the same time giving herself an education. "She learned to read and write all by herself" as an adult, Fidel once remarked. "I don't remember her ever having a teacher other than herself."[6]

FIDEL IS BORN

Fidel Alejandro Castro Ruz, a strapping ten-pound baby, was born in his parents' house on August 13, 1926. (Following Spanish and Cuban custom, his full name includes his mother's maiden surname, although he is generally known by his father's surname only.)

Evidence suggests that people in rural Cuba in the 1920s were generally quite tolerant of illegitimacy, and Fidel does not seem to have been discriminated against because he was born out of wedlock. In any case, it is unlikely that many would have dared to openly insult a wealthy family such as the Castros.

At about age six, Fidel was baptized as a Roman Catholic. He was named for his godfather, one of Ángel's friends. The name Fidel refers to the quality of faithfulness or fidelity. Years later, Castro remarked that it fit him well: "Some have religious faith, and others have another kind. I've always been a man of faith, fidelity, and optimism."[7]

Fidel grew up in an atmosphere of privilege. As the son of a well-known man, he was lavished with attention wherever he went. At home, meanwhile, the boy had every advantage. He was spoiled by his doting mother, was given almost everything he wanted, and—unlike many of the children in the region—always had plenty to eat. Quirk writes, "His first five years were, by all counts, the happiest time of his life."[8]

BOYHOOD

Fidel grew to become a tall, athletic, and adventurous boy. As he got older, he sometimes worked in the family's sugarcane fields. However, he spent most of his time pursuing leisure activities: riding horses, swimming, running with his dogs, playing games, or exploring the family estate.

In addition to being physically energetic, Fidel was gregarious, curious, and outgoing. For instance, he loved to visit the sea, some twenty-five miles away from Las Manacas. He would sit for hours with the fishermen who lived in Oriente's small coastal villages, listening to them tell stories about the ocean.

He also liked to play with other kids. Many of these playmates were the children of his father's employees—poor

---

EARLY DAMAGE?

In his biography Fidel Castro, *Robert E. Quirk quotes a fellow student at the Colegio Belén on the future leader, who tended to be an introverted loner who seemed uncomfortable at parties:*

I think that the worst damage Fidel's parents did him was to put him in a school of wealthy boys without Fidel's being *really* rich, and more than that, without having a social position. With Fidel's kind of maturity, when he grew from a child into an adult, I think that this influenced him, and he had hatred against society people and monied [rich] people.

Haitian workers who toiled in the sugar-cane fields. Fidel's playmates evoked in him his first inklings of social injustice.

Even as a child, he says, he was intensely aware of the differences between his circumstances and those of others. He once remarked to a friend, "I was born into a family of landowners in comfortable circumstances. . . . Everyone lavished attention on me, flattered, and treated me differently from the other boys we played with. . . . These other children went barefoot while we wore shoes."[9]

Fidel's observations of such differences no doubt shaped the ideals he developed as an adult about equality among social classes. He once commented, "Who had to explain a society divided into classes and the exploitation of man by man to me, since I'd seen it all with my own eyes?"[10]

Despite such sensitivity, Fidel was not above occasionally playing the role of a spoiled, arrogant rich kid. If he was losing in a baseball game, for instance, he would sometimes quit and irritably take all the equipment away. After all, it belonged to him.

FRESH SCHOOLBOY

At the age of four, Fidel began attending the local elementary school, which was housed in a one-room schoolhouse on his father's property. He was bright, highly verbal, and quick to learn, but indifferent to any field of study that bored him.

Fidel was never afraid to talk back to his teachers. This was perhaps due to a combination of his natural verbosity and an awareness of his position as a Castro son. As a result, he was often an impertinent and irreverent pupil. He later recalled,

> I spent most of my time being fresh. . . . I remember that whenever I disagreed with something the teacher said to me, or whenever I got mad, I would swear at her and immediately leave school, running as fast as I could.

> One day, I had just sworn at the teacher, and was racing down the rear corridor. I took a leap and landed on a board from a guava-jelly box with a nail in it. As I fell, the nail stuck in my tongue.

> When I got back home, my mother said to me: "God punished you for swearing at the teacher." I didn't have the slightest doubt that it was really true. . . .

> I had one teacher after another, and my behavior was different with each one. . . . With the teacher who treated us well and brought us toys, I remember being well behaved. But when pressure, force or punishment was used, my conduct was entirely different.[11]

MORE SCHOOLING

When he was six, Fidel was sent away to continue his studies. He went to Santiago, the nearest large city and the capital of Oriente.

At first, Fidel hated his time there. Life in Santiago was a rude awakening for him. At the Castro family home, he had been spoiled by his parents and fawned over by those in the community who wanted to curry favor with the Castros. Things were very different in the bigger town.

Fidel lived with his godfather, who was the Haitian consul. At first, the consul and his Cuban wife taught the boy privately. Fidel liked studying certain subjects, including geography and history, especially military history and stories of famous Cuban patriots. He did not like to work hard, however, and he rebelled at rote memorization of subjects he found tedious.

Furthermore, Fidel was homesick. He complained bitterly to his parents by letter about the hardships of life in Santiago. He was especially outraged at how he was treated in his godfather's house. Fidel claimed that his godfather and his wife took money meant for his own room and board and spent it on themselves. He further complained he was fed only tiny portions of very poor quality food.

Eventually, Fidel convinced his parents to let him become a boarder in a more formal school setting. According to one story, when Fidel's parents balked at the expense, he threatened to burn their house down.

LA SALLE

Regardless of whether the arson threat was ever made, Fidel prevailed. He moved out of his godfather's house and enrolled at La Salle. This was a school run by the Christian Brothers, an order of Catholic priests. His younger brother Raúl enrolled there as well.

Being a boarder at school, away from his parents, made a world of difference

---

VIOLENCE AT AN EARLY AGE

In Fidel Castro, *biographer Robert E. Quirk sees a clear link between the adult Castro's love of the military and his boyhood tendency toward violence:*

A clear pattern emerged, from his earliest to his latest pronouncements [speeches], a pattern of death and destruction, of obstinacy, of fighting in the "trenches of the world," of a people, he insisted, willing to die rather than capitulate to any enemy.

From an early age he had exhibited a fascination with violence and with weapons—the larger the better. Not yet ten, he took aim at his mother's chickens with a shotgun. In primary school he pummeled classmates and hit a priest in the stomach. At an elite Jesuit academy he threatened a fellow student with a pistol.

A young Fidel (second from right) poses with classmates at La Salle. Castro regularly picked fights with peers and teachers.

for the outspoken Fidel, who was eager to achieve a level of independence. He later recalled simply: "For me, boarding school meant freedom."[12]

Fidel did not shine academically. He continued to be an indifferent student, demonstrating interest in only a few subjects. Rather, his time at La Salle was marked by the emergence of some of the character traits for which he later became known. In particular, Fidel stood out as aggressive, fearless, and temperamental.

He was pushy, always jostling to be the first in everything and constantly

needing to convince others of some viewpoint. He was also defiant, continually getting into fights—verbal or otherwise—with his classmates and teachers. His brother Raúl recalls that "every day, he would fight. He had a very explosive character."[13]

At least in part, Fidel's aggressiveness may have been a reaction to the taunts of his fellow students. They were, for the most part, the sons of Santiago's aristocrats. Castro recalled in many interviews that these boys mercilessly teased him because of his rough country ways and strong accent.

THE JESUITS

In his fifth year of formal schooling, Fidel transferred to another school, the Dolores, which was also in Santiago. This school was run by another order of Catholic priests, the Jesuits.

The Jesuits were, and still are, renowned for their excellence in teaching. Their centuries-old traditions emphasize such qualities as a comprehensive classical education, spiritual exploration, physical and mental discipline, and developing one's sense of service and justice.

Fidel did well in this tough but compassionate atmosphere. He remarked many times later in life that the education he received with the Jesuits did much to instill in him a deep appreciation for honor, discipline, personal dignity, and social justice. Because of his training, Castro noted, he could never be a passive observer of wrongdoing: "I reacted [to injustice]; I never resigned myself to abuse and the imposition of things by force."[14]

For Fidel, part of the discipline he learned at the Dolores academy involved budgeting his own spending money. Allowed only a twenty-cent weekly allowance, he customarily saved it for one spree every Sunday. He spent ten cents on the movies, five cents for ice cream afterward, and five cents for his favorite weekly comic book, *El Gorrión* (*The Sparrow*).

"MY GOOD FRIEND ROOSEVELT"

As he grew older, Fidel became more than a rebellious young man. He began to excel as an athlete. He also stood out because of his original turn of mind—and his bold willingness to speak it.

One famous example of this eagerness to make his opinions known involved Fidel's hero Franklin D. Roosevelt, who had become president of the United States in 1933. Fidel admired Roosevelt's innovative, heroic efforts to bring America out of

One of Fidel's earliest heroes was President Franklin D. Roosevelt, who led the United States through the Great Depression.

the Great Depression, when millions of Americans were out of work and desperate for relief.

The boy went so far as to write Roosevelt a letter in broken English. The letter managed to be both humble-sounding and shrewd:

My good friend Roosevelt: I don't know very English, but I know as much as write to you. I like to hear the radio, and I am very happy, because I heard in it, that you will be president of a new era. I am a boy but I think very much but I do not think that I am writting to the President of the United States.

If you like, give me a ten dollars bill green american, in the letter, because never, I have not seen a ten dollars bill green american and I would like to have one of them.[15]

A reply from Roosevelt was posted on the school bulletin board, thanking Fidel for his "letter of support and encouragement." However, the president did not see fit to send a "ten dollars bill green american."

A TASTE OF POLITICS

Of all the subjects he was taught by the Jesuits, Fidel was most interested in Cuban history. He was especially intrigued by José Martí, the writer and activist who was a national hero because of his role in Cuba's struggle for independence from Spain.

After a long career both in Cuba and in exile, Martí died in 1895 on the battlefield, fighting for Cuba's freedom. He became an important symbol for political independence in Cuba and throughout Latin America.

Fascinated, Fidel read everything he could about this hero. In time, Fidel would closely identify himself with Martí, and even see himself almost as a reincarnation of the earlier freedom fighter.

Before that could come about, however, Fidel got his first genuine taste of politics. As a teen, he helped Pedro Emilio, his half brother, run for the office of representative from Oriente.

Fidel's job was to go around the countryside near his father's estate teaching illiterate farmers how to vote—for his brother, of course. He had no special interest in politics then, as he recalled many years later. Fidel did, however, have a powerful reason to help out: "The candidate was my brother and he had promised me a horse if he won in the elections."[16]

STARTING PREP SCHOOL

In 1942, Fidel graduated from the Dolores academy and entered the next phase of his schooling. This was the Colegio Belén, a Jesuit college-preparatory school (or high school) in Havana.

Following Cuban custom of the time, Fidel's sister Ángela moved to Havana with him. He was the favored son seeking an education, and it was her responsibility to take care of him and cater to his every need. Ángela mended Fidel's clothes, cooked his meals, and even cut his fingernails for him.

An aerial photo captures the magnificent architecture of downtown Havana. Castro attended high school at the Colegio Belén in the Cuban capital.

The Belén school was considered the best of its kind in the country. Like other Jesuit institutions, it was a place of serious learning and strict enforcement of rules. All the boys wore uniforms and were required to attend Mass regularly.

By all accounts, however, Fidel was generally indifferent to both strict religious observance and to the tidiness of his uniform. His lack of concern about clean clothes, despite his sister's best efforts, reportedly earned him for a time the nickname *Bola de Churre* (Dirtball).

Fidel's strongest subjects in high school were Spanish, history, geography, and agri-culture. However, he remained a poor student and often neglected his schoolwork.

AN AMAZING MEMORY

Fortunately, Fidel was developing a gift that helped him immensely with his schoolwork: an incredible memory. (This near-photographic memory later helped him in another way: by letting him make speeches lasting several hours without the use of notes.)

Fidel had an amazing ability to quickly memorize entire pages of assigned books.

According to legend, this gift turned into a running contest. Fidel's fellow students would test him by asking a question such as, "What does the sociology text say on page so-and-so?" He would then recite the correct answer, word for word and without error.

Because of this ability, Fidel could ignore his studies until the last moment, then cram quickly to pass exams. Getting a passing grade, he knew, was crucial. His allowance from Ángel would have been cut off at once if his grades dropped.

Castro admitted years later that at one point he cheated to make sure his grades stayed high. He told his teachers that he had lost his report booklet, then filled the second one with consistently good grades and showed it to his father. He recalled, "The other notebook, the one they put the real marks in at school, I signed myself [forging Ángel's signature] and returned to school."[17]

Castro's interest in politics developed at an early age, as this high-school yearbook photo of him delivering a speech suggests.

GRADUATING

At Colegio Belén, Fidel's athletic abilities really blossomed. This did not come easily, however. He was a natural athlete, but he was only one of many good athletes at his school. Fidel achieved prominence by setting for himself a regimen of dogged practice, hard work, and discipline. At one point, for instance, he persuaded the priests to light up the school's outside courts so that he could practice basketball at night.

Fidel's primary sport at the time was basketball, but he also enjoyed baseball, soccer, and boxing. He was the head of the school's hiking club and the captain of its basketball club during his senior year. At the age of eighteen, during his senior year, he was named Cuba's outstanding high school athlete.

Fidel could probably have pursued a career as a professional athlete. However, he had already decided that his future was not as a sports star. He was more interested in politics, and he set a goal for himself: to become the successor to his idol, José Martí. As a first step in that direction, he chose to become a lawyer.

When Fidel graduated in 1945, his final school report sounded a prophetic note about his intentions. It said, in part,

> He always distinguished himself in all subjects related to arts and letters. An excellent student and member of the congregation, he was an outstanding athlete, always courageously and proudly defending the school's colors. He won the admiration and affection of all. He will study law, and we have no doubt that he will make a brilliant name for himself. Fidel has what it takes and will make something of himself.[18]

In honor of his graduation, Fidel's father presented him with a good watch. Later that year, after a stay at Las Manacas, Fidel returned to Havana in a new Ford his father also bought for him. He had enrolled in law school.

Chapter 2

Student, Lawyer, and Rebel

Castro's experiences at the law school of the University of Havana were unlike anything he had yet undergone. Life on campus was violent and unpredictable, despite the placid appearance of its elegant, neoclassical setting in the city center.

In theory, the elected heads of the student unions ran most of the university's activities. In practice, however, much of campus life was controlled by bands of young men who called themselves "action groups" but who were little more than gangs of hoodlums.

While some of these men were bona fide students, others were only marginally connected to the university. They spent most of their time harassing students with threats of violence, fixing grades, monopolizing sales of textbooks, and otherwise wreaking havoc.

Castro quickly discovered he needed to plunge into this volatile scene to make his mark. Since the university had no athletic program, he could not stand out on athletic abilities alone. Very soon after his arrival, therefore, he ran for office and was pleased to be elected to the main student union.

During his years at university, Castro's awareness of social injustice strengthened. He became deeply committed to changing Cuba's political structure through legal means and, if necessary, armed revolution. Writer Greg Tozian notes, "The violent, politically charged atmosphere of the University of Havana . . . was the real breeding ground for his career as charismatic leader and fearless defender of Cuban nationalism."[19]

POLITICS

Castro quickly emerged as a figure in national politics as well as a leader on campus. He became an early supporter of a party formed by the reform-minded congressman Eduardo (Eddie) Chibás. This was the Ortodoxos (Orthodox) Party, also called the Cuban People's Party. The Ortodoxos opposed the Autentico Party, Cuba's then-current ruling party, which was led by the corrupt Ramón Grau San Martín.

Castro quickly emerged as a major spokesman against government greed and corruption. He honed his speaking skills—skills that would soon mesmerize a nation—with frequent speeches on behalf of the Ortodoxos. He recalled, "I spoke out against injustice, poverty, unemployment, high rent, the eviction of farmers, low wages, political corruption and ruthless exploitation everywhere."[20]

The tall, handsome student worked hard to project a serious image when appearing in public. Going against Cuba's generally informal customs, Castro almost always wore a suit and tie. Even more strikingly, he did not drink, sing, or dance, which was extremely unusual behavior for a male Cuban. Noting that Castro was thinking ahead in cultivating this image of himself as a serious, single-minded reformer, biographer Tad Szulc writes, "It was all part of his myth-building."[21]

Castro spent long hours furthering his pet causes, and his social life consisted only of political meetings. Furthermore, because he rarely had time for classes, his studies suffered.

THE DOMINICAN AFFAIR

Castro's life was not all political meetings, however. In 1947, he got a taste of armed revolution. This happened when he participated in an unsuccessful attempt to forcibly oust Generalissimo Rafael Trujillo,

Cuban president Ramón Grau addresses a crowd in 1944. When Castro participated in an attempt to overthrow the dictator of the Dominican Republic, Grau retaliated.

the dictator of the Dominican Republic, a nation on the nearby Caribbean island of Hispaniola.

The United States, which was supporting Trujillo, wanted the revolutionaries stopped. The United States put pressure on Cuban president Ramón Grau, who sent a gunboat to capture the attackers and return them to Cuba.

According to some sources, Castro jumped ship as his boat was being brought back into Cuban waters. He swam to shore and took refuge near his home in the village of Birán until he felt safe enough to return to Havana.

The Dominican affair had been a total failure. However, it whetted Castro's appetite for armed action. Military affairs would prove to be an enduring love for him. Historian Clive Foss notes, "The aborted expedition gave Fidel a first taste of military uniforms, weapons and adventure."[22]

Violence, or at least accusations of it, also touched Castro's involvement with politics at home. During the elections of 1948, the police suspected Castro when another student leader was fatally shot. Castro was arrested and briefly held in custody but never charged.

MORE ARMED CONFLICT

A second taste of overseas armed conflict came in that same year. Castro participated in urban riots that broke out in Bogotá, the capital of Colombia, during a high-level conference of Western Hemisphere diplomats.

Juan Perón, the dictator of Argentina, was eager to disrupt these talks. He hoped to foster riots that would humiliate his enemy, the United States. Perón therefore paid a number of Cuban students, including Castro, to stage an anti-American demonstration during the meeting.

The event took a violent turn when a charismatic and popular Colombian labor leader named Gaitán was assassinated during the conference. Days of rioting fol-

---

MARATHON TALKER

Journalist Lee Lockwood, in his book Castro's Cuba, Cuba's Fidel, *evokes the legendary speaking abilities Castro developed as a student and lawyer:*

A conversation with Castro is an extraordinary experience and, until you get used to it, a most unnerving one. In the first place, unless you are very firm, it is seldom properly a conversation at all, but something more like an extended lecture with occasional questions from the audience. . . . A ten-word question can program him for an answer lasting fifteen or twenty minutes. His mind is as precise and organized as a watch and ticks out its ideas just as inexorably.

lowed, during which Castro led groups of angry Colombians into the streets to storm armories and seize weapons. When the riots quieted down, Castro and the other Cubans were smuggled home by the Cuban ambassador.

Castro later claimed that he did not plan beforehand to create armed conflict. He said that joining in the riots was simply a spur-of-the-moment decision created by a sense of justice. "Naturally, I knew that the people were oppressed and were right to rebel; I also knew that Gaitán's death was a terrible crime. So I took sides [and] when I saw the crowd on the move, I joined them."[23]

MARRIAGE

Castro did take occasional breaks from the political life. For one thing, he still loved to play baseball. According to legend, two major-league American teams scouted Castro, and one even offered him a contract. He turned it down with the

The Chrysler Building towers above an elevated train in this 1948 photo of New York City, the place where Castro spent his honeymoon.

excuse that he wanted to complete his studies. These stories have never been definitively proven, however.

Castro also paused long enough to court and marry Mirta Díaz-Balart. Mirta, a blond, green-eyed student at the university, was the sister of Castro's friend Rafael Díaz-Balart. Her father was a prominent member of society; he was the personal lawyer of Fulgencio Batista, Cuba's former president, and later served as interior minister when Batista regained power.

Fidel and Mirta married in the fall of 1948. Because of her family connections and prestige, the event was noted in the society pages of Havana's upper-class newspaper.

Castro's involvement with violent politics affected even his wedding day. Because campus gangs had recently threatened him, the groom wore his pistol to the altar.

The couple enjoyed a lengthy honeymoon, paid for by Mirta's father. They spent several months in New York City, where Castro took an English-language class.

The young man was by this point already critical of the United States, especially its aggressive actions in Latin America. However, Castro also admired many things about the United States.

He loved the grandness of New York City and considered staying on to study at Columbia University. He was also not above spending some of his honeymoon money on an American car: a beautiful white Lincoln Continental. And, of course, there was his lifelong love for baseball, America's national sport.

FROM SCHOOL TO LAW OFFICE

When Fidel and Mirta returned to Havana, they settled into a small apartment and Fidel resumed his studies. Their son Fidelito was born in 1949.

Castro's obsession with politics affected his new responsibilities as a family man. For one thing, he was an unemployed student and there was never enough money. Foss writes, "He gained more popularity than income, but he never had any interest in money. Also he had a wife, who was not pleased to find the furniture repossessed for non-payment, or to have to borrow money from friends to buy milk for the child. Fidel had other cares."[24]

Furthermore, Castro was rarely home. He frequently neglected his family in favor of attending meetings. When he did come home, he often brought a large group of friends with him and insisted that Mirta feed them.

Castro's long-neglected studies needed attention now. He had to cram for his law exams if he hoped to pass. Fortunately, his excellent memory allowed him to cram two years' worth of work into six months, and he graduated in September 1950.

Opening a small law practice with two partners, Castro dedicated himself to serving the poorest citizens of Havana and to righting injustices. His clients often paid him not with money but with produce or chickens—if they paid him at all.

RISING IN THE RANKS

Not only were his clients impoverished, but they were also few in number. Havana had plenty of lawyers, and Castro was not an especially good one. His friends joked that he should have been a good lawyer, because he liked to talk. But he was bored with the details of law practice, of running an office and shepherding cases through the court system.

Most of his energy still went to politics, and he steadily rose within the Ortodoxos Party. Even before graduating, Castro had become the party's second most important person after its founder, Eddie Chibás.

Castro rose still further after a bizarre incident in the summer of 1950. During a radio show, Chibás announced that he could not produce evidence against an education minister whom he had earlier accused of corruption. He proclaimed, "This is my last knock to awaken the civic conscience of the Cuban people,"[25] and then shocked everyone by shooting himself in the stomach.

Ironically, Chibás was unaware that, because he had only paid for twenty min-utes of airtime, his microphone had already been turned off. Only the studio audience witnessed his melodramatic gesture.

Chibás did not die immediately. In the meantime, Castro was constantly at his bedside in the hospital; when the older politician died, eleven days after shooting himself, Castro dominated the eulogies at the memorial service. Chibás's death made Castro the primary figure in the Orto-doxos Party, and thus Cuba's leading opposition voice.

LEGAL BATTLE

Castro planned to run for Chibás's seat in the next general election. However, in 1952 Fulgencio Batista, who had for some time influenced Cuban politics from behind the scenes, staged a bloodless coup to put himself in power. One of his first acts was to dissolve the National Congress (the legislature) and call off the elections.

WHAT HE'S NOT INTERESTED IN

Castro was once asked what motivates him. His reply appears in Jeffrey M. Elliot and Mervyn M. Dymally's 1986 book-long interview session Fidel Castro: Nothing Can Stop the Course of History:

That's too broad a question. It would almost be necessary to write a book to answer all that, my motivations. [Laughter] I'll try to answer.

First, let me state those things that do not motivate me. Material goods do not motivate me. Money does not motivate me. The lust for glory, fame, and prestige does not motivate me. I really think ideas motivate me.

Fearing for his safety in the wake of this coup, Castro went briefly into hiding. On his return, he filed a brief in court. It charged that Batista's takeover violated the Cuban constitution. The high court rejected this petition, however.

Castro's failed attempt to change the government by legal means was deeply frustrating. He gradually became convinced that violent revolution was the only answer. While maintaining a high profile as a peaceful reform spokesman, Castro secretly began assembling a small army of revolutionaries.

In classic revolutionary fashion, Castro formed a central core of himself and a few others, then built "cells" of recruits around this core. These larger groups were structured to ensure secrecy, by keeping the identities of all members unknown to any one individual. If one person were to be captured, he or she would not be able to provide more than a few names even if tortured.

While building this secret army, Castro continued to use whatever nonviolent, legal weapons he had. He realized these could be useful, if only for their publicity value. Foss writes that Castro was convinced "that armed struggle was the only real route to change; but he also used the law. . . . He knew such attacks [as legal briefs] could not succeed, but they guaranteed publicity."[26]

MONCADA BARRACKS

By the end of 1952, Castro later claimed, his group of revolutionaries had about twelve hundred members. Other sources say that the real number was much smaller.

Its core, besides Castro, included Abel and Haydée Santamaria, who were brother and sister. Another prominent member was Naty Revuelta, the wife of a distinguished Havana doctor. This socialite threw herself into the cause, selling jewels to raise money and hiding weapons in her house.

Castro created the army's plan of attack. Some members would remain in Havana and conduct small-scale disruptions, such as setting off bombs in public places. Meanwhile, 165 soldiers would storm Moncada Barracks, near Santiago, and seize the armory's guns. The plan was to distribute these weapons to the people of Oriente, whom Castro felt were naturally rebellious and ready for a fight.

"We had no money," he recalled years later. "But I said to my associates that we didn't have to import weapons from the outside, that our weapons were here, well oiled and cared for, in the stockades of Batista. It was in order to get hold of some of those weapons that we attacked the Moncada Barracks."[27]

"HISTORY WILL ABSOLVE ME"

The attack on July 26, 1953, was a disastrous failure. Half of the hopelessly outnumbered revolutionaries were killed: some in the siege, and many from torture or execution after being captured. Years later, Castro recalled simply, "We were a little too confident. We underestimated the enemy."[28]

A massive crowd gathers in Havana on the tenth anniversary of the attack on Moncada Barracks. The attack was a failure, but it brought Castro celebrity status.

Fidel and Raúl Castro were among those captured and put on trial. Batista feared the publicity of an open trial, however, since Fidel was such a prominent figure. Instead, the revolutionary was tried in a hospital room away from the other prisoners.

Castro was his own lawyer, mounting a vigorous argument without notes. His hours-long summation speech argued that it was legitimate for the Cuban people to rebel against corruption and tyranny. This speech, which came to serve as Castro's revolutionary manifesto, con-

cluded: "I know that imprisonment will be as hard for me as it ever has been for anyone—filled with cowardly threats and wicked tortures. But I do not fear prison, just as I do not fear the fury of the miserable tyrant who snuffed life out of seventy brothers of mine. Sentence me; I don't mind. History will absolve me."[29]

"WHAT WOULD KARL MARX SAY!"

Fidel and Raúl were sentenced to fifteen years each. They were sent to the Machado

THE SEEDS OF HIS THOUGHT

Castro saw the famous speech he gave at his trial as the basis for all his future revolutionary activity. In this excerpt from Lee Lockwood's book Castro's Cuba, Cuba's Fidel, *he comments:*

My political ideas of that time were expressed in the speech to the court during the trial over the Moncada affair, "History Shall Absolve Me." Even then I analyzed the class composition of our society, the need to mobilize the workers, the farmers, the unemployed, the teachers, the intellectual workers, and the small proprietors against the regime. Even then I proposed a program of planned development for our economy, utilizing all the resources of the country to promote its economic development. My Moncada speech was the seed of all the things that were done later on.

prison on a remote island south of the eastern tip of Cuba.

Castro was allowed to receive mail and occasional visitors. He cooked his own meals, something he enjoyed and took pride in. Mostly, however, he read. He asked everyone to send him books, and he spent long hours reading and reflecting. Castro later recalled, "There weren't enough books there for the fifteen or sixteen hours a day that I read."[30]

He educated not only himself, but also the men imprisoned with him, setting up a "school" that met five days a week to discuss politics and other subjects. His favorite topic became Marxism, Karl Marx's socialist ideology that became the foundation of communism. Castro had been exposed to Marxism before, but he studied this philosophy seriously for the first time while in jail.

All in all, life in prison had its pleasures. Castro wrote in a letter, "Mornings,

when I sit outside in the sun, wearing my shorts, enjoying the sea breezes, I think I'm at the beach. Later, back here, I pretend I'm in a little restaurant. People will think I'm on vacation! What would Karl Marx say about such revolutionaries!"[31]

DEFIANT

Despite Castro's ability to keep his spirits up, life in Machado was difficult, and the prisoners remained defiant. When Batista visited in early 1954, Castro and his men greeted the dictator by loudly singing their revolutionary anthem. The rebel leader was given forty days of solitary confinement as punishment for this insult.

He was defiant in other ways as well. Castro discovered, for instance, that he could sneak letters past the jail's censors.

He and his men would hide messages inside cigar boxes or use secret writing between the lines of normal letters. (The "invisible ink" they used was urine or lemon juice; heat from an iron made the writing readable.) Castro's "History Will Absolve Me" speech, reconstructed from memory, reached the outside world in this way.

Surprisingly, the quiet and reflective life suited Castro, who had always been a man of quick action. He wrote to his brother Ramón, "I read a lot and study a

Castro diligently studied the socialist philosophy of Karl Marx (pictured) during his prison sentence.

lot. It seems incredible, but the hours pass as though they were minutes, and I who am of a restless temperament spend my days reading, scarcely moving at all. . . . When one's motives are lofty and great, then [jail] is an honorable place."[32]

OUT OF PRISON

Cuba's most famous political prisoner did not serve his full term. He was released in 1955, after less than two years. Batista pardoned Castro because he wanted to show that he no longer felt threatened by the revolutionary leader.

Castro immediately moved back to Havana. His personal life had changed dramatically while he was in prison. While there, he had discovered that Mirta had taken a job with Batista's interior ministry. Furious that she had, in effect, betrayed him politically, Castro filed for divorce.

If Castro was heartbroken at this turn of events, he did not show his emotions publicly. He wrote to his sister Lidia, "Do not be concerned with me; you know I have a steel heart and I shall be dignified until the last day of my life."[33]

Now, back in Havana, Castro shared an apartment with Lidia, who took care of his needs. He also embarked on a series of affairs with various women. One was his longtime supporter Naty

"SEND ME A SHIRT AND TIE FOR THE TRIAL"

Castro was a prolific letter writer while imprisoned in the 1950s. This excerpt from a letter to his wife, Mirta, is reprinted in Robert E. Quirk's biography Fidel Castro. *The letter included a request for novels, books of philosophy and Shakespeare, and the postscript "Send me a belt."*

I don't know if you are in Oriente or in Havana. I have heard little from you, only that you were in Santiago because of my arrest, and also that you came to the jail to bring me some clothes. I'm all right. You know that prison bars can't affect my spirit, my soul, my conscience. . . .

Write me at the prison and tell me where the boy is and how he is. . . . Take my blue suit to the cleaners and later send me a shirt and tie for the trial. Keep calm and have courage. We have to think above all else about Fidelito. . . . When you come, bring him with you. Surely, they will let me see him.

Revuelta. Even though she was still married to her doctor husband, in 1956 Naty bore Castro a daughter, Alina Fernandez. (Fernandez was the doctor's family name.)

RAILING AGAINST BATISTA

Castro also resumed his schedule of writing, speaking, and broadcasting anti-Batista messages. Life under Batista was terrible for the average Cuban, and Castro had much to rail against.

More than six hundred thousand people were unemployed. About 3.5 million, over half the total population, lived in slums without electricity. For Cuba's elite, however, things got better and better. New skyscrapers went up in Havana to house them. Luxury gambling casinos and hotels catered to the wealthy tourists who came to the city for pleasure. Havana had more Cadillacs per capita than anywhere in the world.

Castro discovered that in his absence he had become a celebrity, and many Cubans were sympathetic to his cause. Years of corruption had made the Cubans cynical and ready for a change. They were eager to embrace Castro's charismatic personality and his revolutionary group—now known as the 26th of July Movement, after the date of the Moncada attack.

Because the Moncada disaster and his imprisonment had turned him into a celebrity, creating for him a hugely sympathetic following, Castro came to regard his failure at Moncada as a political victory. Writer Guillermo Cabrera Infante notes, "The Moncada attack . . . was a failure from the military point of view. But it was a resounding political success."[34]

EXILE

Castro's outspokenness continued even as Batista steadily cracked down on anti-government activity. *Fidelistas*, as Castro's supporters were called, were regularly arrested or harassed, and several of the magazines for which he wrote were forcibly closed.

In the summer of 1955, Castro decided that Batista's repression had become too strong. He exiled himself to Mexico, announcing, "I am leaving Cuba because all doors to peaceful struggle are closed to me." He added ominously, "From trips such as this, one does not return or else one returns with the tyranny beheaded at one's feet."[35]

In Mexico City, Castro lived in a succession of cheap hotels and boarding houses. Every day, he met with an array of Cuban exiles and Mexican leftists. He hoped both to find people willing to join his cause and to raise money for another armed attack on Cuba.

Within two weeks of his arrival in Mexico, Castro met someone who would become a pivotal figure in his life. Ernesto "Che" Guevara, who became the second most important person in the Cuban Revolution, was an Argentine doctor turned full-time revolutionary.

He and Castro talked through the night when they met and afterward were inseparable. Tozian comments, "[T]he two men, filled with revolutionary passion, became immediate friends."[36] They soon assumed nearly equal status in leading the growing band of revolutionaries.

Unlike the more instinctive and intuitive Castro, Guevara was an intellectual who used logic and reason to persuade people to accept his beliefs. The personalities of the two complemented each other well: Guevara was the theoretician and Castro the man of direct, vigorous action. Castro recalled years later, "I believe that at the time I met Che Guevara he had a greater revolutionary development, ideologically speaking, than I had. From the theoretical point of view he was more formed, he was a more advanced revolutionary than I was."[37]

TRAINING

In the fall of 1955, Castro made a fund-raising trip to the United States. Speaking before audiences composed mainly of Cubans and Cuban Americans in Miami and New York, he boldly declared that Cuba would be free—or his men would be dead—by the end of 1956.

Returning to Mexico, Castro resumed recruiting for, and training, his army. Despite his fund-raising efforts, the group had little money. Nonetheless, Castro managed to buy an isolated farmhouse outside Mexico City where they could train in secrecy.

He insisted the group conduct itself with military discipline. They rose at 5 A.M. and walked several miles in small groups to rendezvous points that changed daily for security reasons. They exercised by climbing mountains and rowing on a lake. They practiced firing weapons and improved their agility by playing basketball and soccer.

Life was treacherous for Castro. For one thing, he had to be constantly on the lookout for Batista's spies. Also, money was always extremely tight. This became critical when Castro was arrested for conspiracy; his release, and his continued ability to remain in Mexico, required a series of large bribes.

Castro's private life was also problematic. At one point, he asked Mirta to send their son Fidelito to visit him; he was afraid he might not live to see the boy again. Soon after Fidelito's arrival in Mexico City, however, the boy was kidnapped by members of Mirta's family. He was returned to his mother, who then fled Cuba with him and settled in Spain.

SAILING TO THE REVOLUTION

In the fall of 1956, Castro reached a turning point in his fund-raising efforts. He met with the politician whom Batista had deposed, former president Carlos Prío Socarrás. Prío was rich and eager to see Batista fall. He gave Castro $50,000 in cash.

Castro used the money to buy a fifty-six-foot wooden yacht, the *Granma*. He then brought his men to the Mexican coast and prepared to sail for Cuba.

Eighty-two men—plus weapons, ammunition, and supplies—were crammed into a boat designed to hold only a few people. Despite the dangerous overloading, the *Granma* left Mexico in December 1956.

Bad weather, mechanical problems, and serious seasickness among the men made the crossing hellish, and it took much longer than planned. There were further

ANALYZING EVERY WORD

Castro is well known for constantly analyzing everything he says. He reflects on this in a passage from Jeffrey M. Elliot and Mervyn M. Dymally's Fidel Castro: Nothing Can Stop the Course of History:

[Y]ou constantly have to analyze every word you say—every single word—and how you said it, at the moment you said it. You should always analyze what you do. That's why I say you're never quite satisfied. I think such an attitude is useful, it's positive.

It's like when an athlete does something wrong and says to himself: "That was wrong. I have to do better next time." I think [that if] you apply that approach of never being quite satisfied with everything you do, you'll have a formula that, I think, politicians should follow. At least, you have to be on guard against self-complacency and conceit.

EARLY IDEAS

This excerpt from a manifesto written in 1953 shows that Castro's revolutionary ideals were formed years before he took power. It is reprinted in Hugh Thomas's Cuba, or, The Pursuit of Freedom:

The Revolution declares its firm intention to establish Cuba on a plan of welfare and economic prosperity that ensures the survival of its rich subsoil, its geographical position, diversified agriculture and industrialisation. . . .

The Revolution declares its respect for the workers . . . and . . . the establishment of total and definitive social justice, based on economic and industrial progress under a well-organised and timed national plan. . . . The Revolution . . . recognises and bases itself on the ideals of Martí. . . . The Revolution declares its absolute and reverent respect for the Constitution which was given to the people in 1940. . . . In the name of the martyrs, in the name of the sacred rights of the fatherland.

Members of Castro's militia display weapons seized from Batista's army. Castro believed that armed insurrection was the sole means to achieve his revolutionary ideals.

problems when the *Granma* finally made it to Cuba. The boat got stuck in mudflats, the lifeboat was overloaded and sank, and the men had to wade ashore through waist-high water in a mangrove swamp.

No matter. To Castro, this was the beginning of a glorious revolution. Foss writes, "Like José Martí in 1895, he had returned to liberate Cuba."[38] In Castro's mind, Cuba was as good as free.

3 The Revolutionary Triumphs

Two main factors contributed to the dashing of Castro's early dreams of glory. Fulgencio Batista's spies had informed the dictator of the plans for the July 26 insurrection, so his forces were prepared. Also, bad weather kept those *Fidelistas* who were already in Cuba from reaching the war zone in time.

As a result, the tiny rebel army was ambushed and almost completely destroyed within three days of its landing. Castro recalled later, "It was a hard day, a very hard day. The planes caught us by surprise, and it was a miracle that we weren't all wiped out."[39]

BEATING A RETREAT

Only twelve of the eighty-two *Granma* revolutionaries survived. Among them were Castro, Che Guevara, and the leader's brother Raúl. Split into even smaller groups, the dozen rebels retreated into the Sierra Maestra mountain range, which stretches for about one hundred miles along Cuba's southern coast. Castro recalled, "There was a moment when I was Commander in Chief of myself and two others."[40]

The situation was desperate. The surviving rebels had few weapons, little medicine, no permanent shelter, plenty of mosquitoes to torment them, and almost nothing to eat. Each soldier's ration consisted of half a sausage and two dry crackers a day.

The rebels could suck on raw sugarcane for sustenance, but they had to be careful; any chewed pieces they left behind made a perfect trail for Batista's forces, which were still in the area, to follow. On the other hand, Castro's men could beg for food whenever they found a farmer's hut; the *campesinos*, as the farmers were called, were usually sympathetic and willing to feed the rebels when there was something to spare.

Back in Havana, Batista publicly announced that he had crushed the rebellion. He told reporters that all of the insurgents—including Castro—were dead. In the absence of news reports to the contrary, most Cubans believed these official announcements.

CONFIDENCE

The small groups of dispersed soldiers eventually found one another and established

Castro (center) poses with officers of his rebel army at their Sierra Maestra base. The soldiers depended on the support of campesinos *for survival while in the mountains.*

a base in the mountains. Undaunted, Castro set about rebuilding his army. The rugged and remote terrain of the Sierra Maestra made a perfect base for this reconstruction. According to writer Robert E. Quirk, the mountains "offered Castro the protection he required to build the Rebel Army virtually unhindered."[41]

It seemed absurd to think that a dozen soldiers could successfully campaign against an established dictator with a large military force. Nonetheless, Castro's confidence never wavered.

According to one story, when he was reunited with his brother Raúl, Castro asked him, "How many rifles did you bring?" Raúl replied that he had five and Castro exclaimed, "And with the two I have, this makes seven! Now, yes, we have won the war!"[42]

Castro was also confident that the *campesinos* of the Sierra Maestra would help him. The farmers had no money, but he relied on them to lend support in other ways: by feeding his army, smuggling weapons in, and acting as lookouts against further attack. Castro's firm belief was that "no revolutionary movement . . . that is supported by the peasant population can be defeated. Unless naturally, the revolutionary military leaders commit very grave errors."[43]

LOCAL SUPPORT

The most important support that the residents of the Sierra Maestra provided was a supply of new recruits. The rebels apparently had little trouble finding them. A good number of the *campesinos*, as Castro predicted, had no love for the Batista regime in far-off Havana.

They were therefore happy to join a revolution that promised fair-minded, even-handed treatment, even if that revolution seemed hopeless. Writer Greg Tozian notes, "Sugarcane cutters and cigar rollers, once acquiescent, became zealots for the cause of Cuban independence after nearly five hundred years of foreign rule."[44]

In Castro's opinion, this support was inevitable, because the ruling government's brutalities and corruption had made life intolerable. Many years later he commented,

> Batista was . . . a representative of the military caste, of the corrupt politicians, of the big businessmen, of the huge landowners, and of the foreign companies. . . . The only thing he could do was [to] defend those interests by fire and sword.
>
> He had no other choice than to use terror. As the struggle sharpened, he found himself obliged to resort more and more to committing barbarities. And while he was becoming more hated, we were developing more and more support among the population where we were fighting.[45]

"A FEW THOUSAND INDIVIDUALS"

The anthology Fidel: My Early Years, *edited by Deborah Shnookal and Pedro Álvarez Tabío, includes a letter to a friend written from Machado prison in April 1954. This excerpt indicates Castro's cheerful willingness to alienate people if it meant furthering his cause:*

[H]ow pleased I would be to revolutionize this country from top to bottom! I am sure that all the people could be happy—and for them I would be ready to incur the hatred and ill will of a few thousand individuals, including some of my relatives, half of my acquaintances, two-thirds of my professional colleagues, and four-fifths of my former schoolmates.

Rebel Life

By the end of his first year in the mountains, Castro completely controlled a large part of the mountain region. The headquarters of the Free Territory of Cuba, as Castro called this area, was a small town in itself. It included a hospital, a leather workshop, a butcher shop, a cigar factory, and even a newspaper. In the surrounding countryside, meanwhile, Castro organized a system of schools for the *campesinos*.

The rebels, Castro included, lived communally. They ate together. They wore identical military fatigue uniforms. They all slept in hammocks slung in trees or in crude wooden shacks. They rarely bathed, and, because they had no razors, the men (who were in the vast majority) did not cut their hair or shave.

This last trait gave rise to their nickname *los barbudos*—the bearded ones. The uniforms, beards, and long hair were kept long after the rebels had taken over Cuba, as marks of courage. Castro later remarked about that period in his life, "Everyone grew a beard and let their hair grow long. Gradually, these became first an element of identification—the guerilla fighter's identification card—and later a symbol."[46]

Castro insisted the rebels live according to strict military discipline. This was necessary, he said, because of the constant dangers the rebels faced. Their hardships were not always caused by government forces, however. For instance, the deep bites of horseflies caused painful, easily infected wounds. Castro swore this constant plague was as evil an enemy as Batista. Another serious hardship was the lack of proper dental care. Castro himself was nearly always in pain or at least in discomfort.

Guerrilla Army

In time, the number of soldiers under Castro's command grew to at least eight hundred. Some sources say this figure was much higher, perhaps around three thousand.

These recruits were a guerrilla army—that is, soldiers who carry out many small-scale attacks against a larger enemy. Castro's strategy was to wear down his much larger foe by staging unexpected assaults and committing acts of sabotage whenever possible. The element of surprise was crucial here, Castro remarked to a friend: "All my military science can be summed up by the game of Ping-Pong. Return the ball where your enemy least expects it."[47]

It was for this reason that Castro had ordered the first attack on an army stronghold, very soon after the devastating defeat when his group had first landed. Quirk points out that this early assault provided a welcome psychological boost: "After botching the invasion, [Castro] and his men needed a victory to lift their sagging spirits."[48]

It was just such a victory. At the army garrison at La Plata, twenty-eight rebels burned the barracks and seized weapons, ammunition, and food, but suffered no losses. As time went on, they staged more attacks, and often were victorious.

Each victory was small: a handful of guns here, a cache of food there. However, word of the dedicated rebels was beginning to reach the outside world. Furthermore, each attack was magnified by the attention the rebels were beginning to receive across Cuba and even outside the country.

Both the rebels and their leader understood well the value of such media attention. They carefully cultivated relationships with certain journalists, knowing that even the tiniest skirmish could, given the right emphasis, be seen as a glorious triumph. As Guevara observed, "The presence of a foreign journalist, preferably American, was more important for us than military victory."[49]

THE POWER OF PUBLICITY

Throughout 1957, Castro used outside journalists to create interest and sympathy for his cause. One especially influential piece was a *New York Times* article by veteran reporter Herbert Matthews.

After reaching Castro's heavily guarded mountain camp, Matthews published a lengthy, three-part article. It painted Castro in glowing, romantic terms. The journalist made the revolutionary sound like he was a virtual reincarnation of José Martí, a man who represented Cuba's destiny:

> President Fulgencio Batista has the cream of his army around the area, but the army men are fighting a thus-far losing battle to destroy the most dangerous enemy General Batista has yet faced in a long and adventurous career as a Cuban leader and dictator. . . .
>
> [Castro's program] is vague and couched in generalities, but it amounts to a new deal for Cuba. . . .
>
> [T]he personality of [Castro] is overpowering. It is easy to see that his men adored him and also to see why he has caught the imagination of the youth of Cuba.[50]

Che Guevara, Castro's most trusted lieutenant, understood the power of the media to magnify even the most insignificant rebel victory.

During Matthews's interviews, Castro shrewdly found a way to inflate the apparent size of his army. He had Raúl parade the rebel army past the tent where he and Matthews were talking.

Only eighteen men were available, but they marched past Matthews several times. Apparently, the reporter never realized he was seeing the same soldiers. To heighten the illusion, a breathless aide rushed up to Castro at one point to deliver a "message" from a nonexistent second column of soldiers.

SYMPATHY

Matthews's articles caused a sympathetic stir in the United States, but they were a genuine sensation in Cuba. They proved to an astonished Cuba that—contrary to Batista's claim—Castro was alive and well.

Up until this point, Batista had been trying to cut out any references to Castro in foreign newspapers that reached Cuba. This was quite literal; the dictator employed a corps of women with scissors, who snipped out offending articles from each copy of each periodical. Thus, every issue of the *New York Times* in which Matthews's first article appeared had a gaping hole on the front page.

Nonetheless, the article appeared in Cuba. Word of its revelations first arrived in Cuba via Spanish-language radio stations in Miami, and uncensored issues of the newspaper were later smuggled into the country.

It is possible that Castro might have been victorious without such publicity.

However, as Quirk points out, foreign journalists such as Matthews were of invaluable help to Castro in casting himself as a mythic figure: "The American reporter, in only three articles, gave the Cuban people a charismatic leader with whom they could identify, a hero whom they could admire. . . . For more than three decades Fidel Castro's conception of himself and his public demeanor were determined by that image."[51]

SETTING THE PACE

As the undisputed rebel leader, Castro set himself to be a formidable example for his men. He had tremendous energy, going hard for days and sleeping only in short catnaps, even if his energy was expended only in marathon sessions of dominoes, a game he loved to play when rainy weather kept him inside his tent.

Castro also set a standard for his men in military-style precision and discipline. One example of this was his habit (which he maintained for years) of always wearing two watches, so that if one stopped he could still be synchronized with the other rebels.

Furthermore, Castro was a tireless and intrepid hiker who loved to roam the rugged Sierra Maestra. Roberto Salas, a photographer who often accompanied Castro during this period, recalls, "One thing about Fidel . . . that guy never stops. He doesn't stop to drink water. He doesn't stop to go to the bathroom. He covers a lot of ground."[52]

The people to whom Castro was close during his time in the mountains, natu-

FIDEL ON A MULE

Pedro Miret, who had been with Castro in the Sierra Maestra Mountains, one night in 1964 at 3 A.M., after a full day of traveling and working, was watching him play Ping-Pong while lecturing his exhausted audience about crop fertilizers. Quoted in Lee Lockwood's Castro's Cuba, Cuba's Fidel, *Miret comments:*

Look at him. He will be talking until six o'clock. He is just the same now as he was in the Sierra Maestra. The only difference is that in the Sierra he would have looked at his watch and said, "Well, only 3 A.M.—we still have time to walk to the next mountain!" Sometimes in the Sierra it got so bad we had to put Fidel on a mule. Only because the mule walked slower than Fidel.

---

rally enough, were those who were most committed to his cause. They included his longtime colleagues Guevara and Raúl Castro. Another close companion was Celia Sánchez.

CLOSE COMPANIONS

Sánchez was the daughter of a wealthy, radical physician. He had instilled in her a devotion to José Martí and the ideals of Cuban independence. Sánchez had become an early supporter of Castro's revolution, and she was almost certainly his lover for a time as well.

In time, Sánchez became Castro's most trusted aide and companion. One of her main jobs was to find new recruits for the cause and bring them into the fold. Also, since details bored Castro, she took over all his business matters, such as bills and correspondence.

Unlike the sometimes brusque Castro, Sánchez has been described as being an unusually warm person. She was, observers agree, absolutely devoted to Castro, and perhaps the one woman he really needed.

In return, she seemed to need him just as much. French journalist Michel Tourguy, who covered Cuba during the revolution for a French press agency, remarked of Sánchez, "Her saint was Fidel, and she was his muse. It was one of those historic friendships."[53]

ON THE RADIO

As always, Castro was a champion talker during his time in the Sierra Maestra. At first, this took the form of lectures to his men and to local *campesinos*. Early in 1958, however, Castro acquired a short-wave transmitter. This gave him the ability to

Castro uses a short-wave transmitter to broadcast his revolutionary message across Cuba. Radio enabled Castro to promote his cause in the island's urban centers.

broadcast his stirring revolutionary messages across the nation.

On the radio, Castro called for a variety of measures, including freedom for all political prisoners, an end to government corruption, and programs to benefit the Cuban people, such as movements to teach reading and writing.

He denied that the rebels, when and if they were victorious, would take over foreign property. He firmly declared that he was not a Communist. Furthermore, he publicly renounced any desire to be the future leader of Cuba.

Castro used the radio, and his media interviews, to further his cause in Cuba's urban centers. One major push came in the spring of 1958, when Castro called for a national strike.

IN THE CITIES

As part of the strike, Castro ordered all traffic to stop in Cuba's urban centers. He also took such measures as sending parties out to round up cattle on unguarded grazing lands in rural areas. The animals thus gathered—Castro claimed they numbered about ten thousand—were distributed to needy *campesinos*.

Thousands of Cubans heeded Castro's call, and Batista was forced to declare a national emergency. Nonetheless, most

Cubans did not take part in the strike, which in retrospect was poorly planned and hastily executed.

Castro had hoped the strike would depose Batista. However, Batista still had enough support from business and financial leaders to keep it from becoming widespread. Quirk writes, "In the cities and towns of Cuba the strike flickered like a guttering candle."[54]

Meanwhile, there was other anti-Batista action in Cuba's cities. *Fidelistas* in these towns organized bombings and other forms of sabotage. A group in Havana even took over the Havana radio station for a time and boldly attacked the Presidential Palace. The rebels got as far as Batista's office, and he barely escaped. The dictator retaliated by having his army shoot or capture as many of the *Fidelistas* as possible.

"MY TRUE DESTINY"

As his stature and credibility grew, Castro was showing increased signs of a conflicted, muddied relationship with the United States. During his honeymoon with Mirta in America, he had been highly critical of America, while at the same time openly admiring many things about it.

Now, as a guerrilla fighter, Castro had similarly conflicted feelings. According to some sources, the impoverished rebel was willing to accept help from American sources. There is some evidence that he received $50,000 from the Central Intelligence Agency (CIA). Perhaps this was the U.S. government's way of hedging its bets, by offering token support to Castro

without the knowledge of the increasingly shaky Batista regime. Castro was beginning to look like a winner, and the Americans may have felt it made sense to have him in their debt. The CIA, however, has always denied any such donation.

In any event, Castro was entertaining frequent anti-American thoughts. He still mistrusted the larger country, which he feared would not readily give up its Cuban interests. After the rebels had withstood a rocket attack by Batista's forces using U.S.-built fighters, Castro wrote to Celia, "I have sworn that the Americans will pay very dearly for what they are doing. When this war has ended, a much bigger and greater war will start for me, a war I shall launch against them. I realize that this will be my true destiny."[55]

FINAL OFFENSIVE

The rocket attack was just one of many attempts by Batista to crush the rebels. After many such failures, the dictator decided in May 1958 to mount a major offensive. Seven to ten thousand troops and an air force were dispatched to the Sierra Maestra, armed with U.S.-made weapons and planes.

What followed—an arduous seventy-six-day offensive—ended in failure for the government. The many thousands of well-armed soldiers under Batista were unable to rout Castro's several hundred poorly armed guerrillas.

Biographer Tad Szulc notes that Castro's army was simply better equipped for

In a 1934 ceremony, Batista proudly displays medals identifying him as the head of Cuba's military. Batista ordered several unsuccessful offensives to destroy Castro's rebels.

that particular region and set of circumstances. He writes,

> Batista had crushing superiority in numbers and firepower, but Castro had turned the mountains into a fortress he could defend with a much smaller force, men who knew every path in the forest, every turn of the road, and every peasant's house in the immensely complicated terrain.[56]

In the wake of this failed offensive, support for Batista, both within and outside

Cuba, collapsed quickly. The United States, the dictator's most important political ally, had been supplying him with guns and other war material. Now it withdrew this support, just in time to be able to make the claim that it was remaining neutral in the conflict.

HAVANA FALLS

After Batista's offensive failed, Castro launched a major attack of his own late in

1958. Moving boldly out of the mountains, he captured Palma Soriano, a strategic town, and made steady progress in other parts of Cuba.

In some ways, the battle proved easier than expected. Many of Batista's soldiers were sympathetic to the rebel cause and surrendered immediately when confronted. Also, the fighting was not always fierce. The rebels were able to take time out, for instance, to listen to radio broadcasts of the World Series. Castro's command post,

A NATIONAL FIESTA

The celebratory atmosphere across Cuba following Batista's flight from power is described in Robert E. Quirk's book Fidel Castro:

Convinced at last that the reports were true, the Cubans began to celebrate the fall of the dictator. In the suburbs initially, and then in the center of the capital, they formed impromptu motorcades through the narrow streets of the city. Everywhere there was the tumult of shouting and the honking of horns, and Havana took on the aspects of a national fiesta.

A motorcade of Castro supporters celebrates victory in the streets of Havana after the removal of Batista is announced.

which by that time occupied a country club outside Santiago, was able to use the club's television set to view the last game.

Meanwhile, attacks by the *Fidelistas* in the cities against Batista's forces grew increasingly bold. On New Year's Day 1959, Castro received exciting news from Havana. Batista had fled the country, reportedly taking with him millions of dollars in government money.

Joyful *Habañeros*—residents of Havana—reacted to his departure by dancing in the streets. They also smashed windows in U.S.-owned hotels, destroyed parking meters, and looted the fancy casinos—all hated symbols of the Batista government.

There was, however, remarkably little bloodshed; mostly, it was a nonviolent celebration. *Habañeros* for the most part heeded Castro's repeated radio appeals to avoid bloodshed. Szulc comments, "[F]or three days the capital was without government or authorities; but there was . . . only joy, chanting, and singing into the night."[57]

"THE INVINCIBLE CAPTAIN!"

Castro and his group continued to take more territory and on January 2, 1959, thousands of people jubilantly cheered as they entered the city of Santiago. It was after midnight, but the city's main streets and central plaza were packed as people tried to catch a glimpse of the man one Santiago newspaper described as "Fidel Castro, the invincible captain! The man whose very name is a banner!"[58]

In his speech to this welcoming crowd, Castro declared that the revolution he was promising would make Cuba totally free—not like in 1898, when Spain left and the Americans took over. He further announced, "The revolution begins now."[59]

Castro then began his triumphant six-hundred-mile journey to Havana. Riding in an open jeep, he was part of a long caravan of army tanks, armored cars, and buses. In many towns along the way, Castro stopped to make speeches, which sometimes lasted for four, five, or even six hours.

All along the way, the roadsides filled with excited Cubans. Everyone, it seemed, wanted to see Castro, shake his hand, and kiss or embrace him. The feeling was extraordinary, according to Lee Lockwood, a journalist who accompanied the caravan:

> I doubt if anyone who was present in Cuba then, whether native or foreigner, and regardless of his present opinion of Castro, will ever forget the spirit of exaltation and hope that permeated the island during those first days after the Revolution took power. The Central Highway to the capital was a five-hundred-mile-long parade route, lined a day in advance with Cubans waiting impatiently to catch a glimpse of Fidel as he passed.[60]

IN HAVANA

Castro's reception when he reached Havana on January 8 was no less ecstatic. Crowds shouted *Viva Fidel* ("Long live Fidel") and waved Cuban flags and placards of greeting. At the city's outskirts, Castro found the streets so clogged with well-wishers that he needed a helicopter to reach the center of the city, where he spoke before an estimated half-million people.

In addition to this mammoth welcome, a more personal surprise awaited Castro in Havana. Soon after his arrival, his son Fidelito was brought to him. Mirta was allowing the boy to return to his father's care. Crying, Fidel embraced him and uncharacteristically forgot the speech he had planned to give.

Once the jubilant welcome was over, Castro lost no time in setting up a provisional,

Castro concludes a 1960 speech with the victory sign. Although he insisted he would not hold office in the new government, Castro appointed himself prime minister.

Guillermo Garcia, one of the revolutionaries who was with Castro in the Sierra Maestra Mountains, nearly a decade later spoke in admiration of Castro's ability to learn quickly. The excerpt is from Robert E. Quirk's book Fidel Castro:

Fidel had never been in these mountains before. But in six months he knew the whole Sierra better than any *guajiro* [peasant] who was born there. He never forgot a place that he went. He remembered everything—the soil, the trees, who lived in each house. In those days I was a cattle buyer. I used to go all over the mountains. But in six months Fidel knew the Sierra better than I did, and I was born and raised here.

or temporary, government. At first, his only official role was as commander of the armed forces. Manuel Urrutia Lleó, a moderate judge, served as president, and José Miro Cardona, a lawyer, became prime minister.

Castro repeatedly stated that he was not interested in a leadership role, but whenever he made his frequent impromptu speeches in the streets of Havana, audiences cheered wildly. The charismatic rebel was quickly becoming a popular favorite.

THE NEW LEADER

By February 1959, barely a month into the new regime, Castro replaced Miro as prime minister and also assumed another title: premier. President Urrutia, meanwhile, who proved to be too moderate for Castro, was replaced by another, more sympathetic politician.

The American government had already formally recognized the new Cuban leadership as legitimate. U.S. authorities got a firsthand taste of Castro's charismatic presence when he visited America later that year.

Privately, some American politicians who met Castro thought he seemed overwhelmed by his new role. Christian Herter, then U.S. undersecretary of state, later described him as "a most interesting individual, very much like a child in some ways, quite immature regarding problems of government, and puzzled and confused by some of the practical difficulties now facing him."[61]

Others recognized his potential for playing a major role in world politics. Vice President Richard Nixon noted, "The one fact we can be sure of is that he has those indefinable qualities which make him a leader of men. Whatever we may think of him, he is going to be a great factor in the development of Cuba and very possibly in Latin American affairs generally."[62]

It was a buoyant period for Castro. His tiny band of ragtag guerrillas had conquered a well-trained and well-armed force many times its size. He became what he had always dreamed: the liberator of his country. He became, despite his repeated denials of interest, the nation's leader.

Soon, however, the celebrations ended. It was time to start the serious business of running a country—and transforming it through revolutionary ideas.

4 *El Líder Máximo*

The task of reforming the Cuban government was far more complex and exasperating than Castro had imagined. He responded to the challenge with vigor, but complained at one point to a colleague that he felt like he was still aboard the yacht *Granma*, trying to seal a nonstop series of leaks: "The more problems we solve, the more problems appear."[63]

He immediately enacted many moderate reforms, including rent cuts for poor city dwellers and programs to build homes, hospitals, and schools in the countryside. Castro also ordered the construction of hundreds of miles of roads, outlawed prostitution and gambling, stepped up industrialization, and began his push for free medical care.

MODERATE REFORMS

One of Castro's most successful programs was a literacy movement. Under it, the percentage of illiterate Cubans dropped within five years from 25 percent to 3 percent. This was an issue close to Castro's heart. Remarking that every-one should have the opportunities that reading provides, he said, "If I hadn't been able to read and write, what role could I have played in the history of my country, in the revolution?"[64]

There was a darker side to Castro's sweeping new reforms. He retaliated against Batista-era politicians, trying hundreds of them in court on charges of crimes, such as assassination, treason, and corruption. At least seventy Batista cronies were executed and many more were imprisoned. To this day, Castro has never abandoned the tactic of imprisoning those who oppose the revolution.

Meanwhile, revolutionaries—most of them lacking in relevant experience—replaced these career politicians. Among them were Raúl Castro, who commanded the military, and Che Guevara, who became both minister of industry and head of the national bank.

Castro was unapologetic about placing such colleagues in important positions. He commented about the revolutionaries who had served with him in the Sierra Maestra, "These are my friends whom I can trust. They were my companions when I was in danger."[65]

FROM MODERATE TO RADICAL

Moderate reforms were only the beginning. Castro had more radical programs in mind. To fulfill them, he decreed, Cuba needed a one-party government with complete control over housing, health care, education, road building, and all other areas of political and cultural life. Castro banned elections, saying that the country was not yet ready for democracy. Instead, his government would control everything.

Throughout the 1960s, it directed a series of radical experiments that were extensions of the leader's will. Robert E. Quirk points out that these programs shifted with Castro's whims: "Fidel Castro's fertile imagination conceived many plans to bring instant prosperity to the Cuban people, and he threw himself into each new scheme with unbridled enthusiasm. Whatever the project, Cuba would be the best in the world, make the best in the world, do the best in the world."[66]

The broadest of these experiments took large tracts of Cuba's farmland from their owners, who often lived overseas, and gave them to the peasants who actually worked on them. To Castro, this agrarian

Cuban schoolgirls share drawings. Castro made education one of his government's top priorities, and Cuba now enjoys one of the world's highest literacy rates.

reform, *la reforma agraria*, was the cornerstone of his revolution: "It means the quickest satisfaction of the fundamental needs of the people: food, clothing, and shelter. It means the immediate utilization of the major natural resources which our country possesses."[67]

The land was organized into collective farms, or cooperatives, which were overseen by Castro's National Institute for Agrarian Reform. Some small farms remained intact, but eventually, Castro hoped, all of Cuba's farmland would come under government authority. The collective farms were ordered to grow many different kinds of food in an attempt to diversify Cuba's production and wean the nation away from its dependence on sugarcane.

Land reform quickly assumed an enormous role in Cuban life. The slogan "Agrarian reform works" was repeated endlessly on television and radio. The nation's phone operators were even required to answer calls by repeating it.

AMONG MANY *FIDELISTAS,* SOME DISSIDENTS

Millions of Cubans not only welcomed such sweeping changes, but also came

---

A HUNGRY GUY

Castro's appetite is enormous, in keeping with his legendary energy. In this passage from Lee Lockwood's Castro's Cuba, Cuba's Fidel, *the journalist describes a celebratory feast:*

Beginning with a jar of yogurt (which, he says, he learned to like in Russia because "it prepares the stomach"), he devours a full meal of roast pig, fried chicken, rice, fou-fou (a starchy fruit of the banana family, indigenous to the region, which is rolled into heavy, sticky balls, the size of matzoh balls, then boiled), malanga (a starchy vegetable something like boiled, mashed white turnips), ham-and-cracker sandwiches, tomato slices and lettuce salad.

Then, just when we are all gasping and looking forward to coffee and cigars, Jose Maria, Fidel's personal army cook, ducks under the tent flap with a gigantic filet mignon spitted on a stick, still sizzling from the fire. He places it on the Jefe's [Chief's] plate. Fidel stares at it for a moment, grimacing. It would make a meal in itself. He pokes it with his fork. At last, heaving a sigh, he cuts into the juicy meat and manages to consume about half of it before satiety forces him to push the dish away and signal for the table to be cleared.

---

close to worshiping their instigator. They posted Castro's portrait everywhere, talked about him constantly, and hung on to every word of his speeches. They called him *El Líder Máximo*—the Maximum Leader—a shining symbol for a new and free Cuba.

Schoolchildren were encouraged to look on the revolution as a glorious event, and on Castro as a father figure to be honored and revered. They chanted slogans such as "Full Support for the Revolution!" and "Fatherland or Death!" Almost every aspect of Cuban life similarly glorified Castro's vision. The first phrase literacy students learned, for instance, was *"la reforma agraria"*; the first full sentence translated to "The *campesinos* work in the cooperative."

Some Cubans, however, objected violently to what was happening. Perhaps they had been prepared for moderate reforms, but not for radical changes. Appalled with Castro's more extreme policies, about 1 million people—roughly 10 percent of the population—fled Cuba between the early 1960s and the early 1980s, with a substantial number settling in Miami, Florida. Embarrassingly for Castro, two of his sisters were among them.

Most of the people who fled belonged to the middle and upper class; many were educated professionals such as engineers, doctors, and lawyers. Castro was, for the most part, happy to see these dissidents go, and at first he made no attempt to stop them. Historian Clive Foss observes, "Dictators often slaughter their opponents. Fidel followed a much cleverer policy. After the first wave of executions, dissidents were free to leave."[68]

SILENCING THE CRITICS

Not all the dissidents left, however; millions who were critical of the revolution chose to remain. Castro systematically set about silencing these critics.

For instance, he had an iron hand regarding counterrevolutionary public demonstrations. The last major demonstration against his policies occurred in 1962, when a group of housewives in the town of Cárdenas marched to protest a lack of food. Castro sent in tanks to disperse them, and the message was clearly heard: Large demonstrations were not allowed.

Also, thousands of people—the estimates vary from twenty thousand to fifty thousand—were imprisoned in the 1960s for alleged counterrevolutionary activities. Castro silenced any radio and television station that dared to be critical, usually by taking them over and turning them into official government stations.

Furthermore, all publications in Cuba had to be approved by the government. The three dozen daily newspapers operating in Cuba before the revolution were gone within a year and a half after being forcibly closed, pressured to fold through lack of advertising, or turned into government-controlled operations that issued only preapproved "news" and sympathetic commentary.

NO RELIGION, NO TRAITORS

One of Castro's most stunning moves, considering Cuba's largely Catholic population, was to ban all religion, on the grounds

Pope John Paul II visits with Castro in 1998. The pope came to the island to improve relations between the Cuban government and the Catholic Church.

that it was counterrevolutionary. Among other measures, Castro shut down religious schools and expelled dozens of priests.

Castro's plan was to replace religion with revolutionary ideals. By Christmas 1960, holy celebrations were officially banned. Instead of traditional Nativity scenes, government workers across the country erected huge images of Fidel, Guevara, and Juan Almeida (another high-ranking revolutionary). They were shown as the three "Wise Men" bearing gifts of agrarian reform, urban reform, and education.

Castro also cracked down on other allegedly counterrevolutionary groups, including rebellious teens and homosexuals. Such groups were severely discriminated against and often sent to brutal institutions called reeducation camps, where they were subjected to harsh attempts to "reform" their lives.

Everyone in the new Cuba was expected to harmonize with Castro's programs. To uncover those who did not, he organized a nationwide network of Committees for the Defense of the Revolution. These were neighborhood groups that pledged to report any suspicious or antirevolutionary behavior.

Thousands of people were arrested because of these informers. Journalist Georgie Anne Geyer notes the irony, considering that Castro had once brutally dealt with informers who betrayed his soldiers in the mountains: "[T]he man who had killed *chivatos* [informers] without a second thought in the Sierra turned the entire Cuban people into a *chivato* nation."[69]

Neighborhood Watchdogs

In 1960, Castro created the Committees for the Defense of the Revolution (CDR). This network of neighborhood watchdogs formed an islandwide system of government investigators that still exists.

Nearly every block in every Cuban city, as well as almost every factory and farm, has a branch of the CDR. Roughly 80 percent of the Cuban population are *Cederistas*, as its members are known. This makes the CDR, taken as a whole, Cuba's single largest organization.

The CDRs fulfill many civic functions. These include blood donation and vaccination campaigns, hurricane evacuation, and anticrime watches.

However, their main function is spying. Each neighborhood group keeps detailed records of every occupant in every house, including school and work history, spending habits, contact with foreigners, and attendance (or nonattendance) at official meetings. The CDRs also inform authorities of any suspicious activity in their neighborhoods, such as the appearance of strangers or someone who privately speaks ill of Castro.

Castro has widely praised the CDRs. In a speech in 2000 (reprinted in Isabel Garcia-Zarza, "Neighborhood Watch Turns 40"), he stated, "The best work the CDRs have done . . . is to have saved the revolution itself."

Critics, however, argue that the CDRs have formed a Big Brother–style spy network that stifles individuality. In his book *Fidel Castro*, Robert E. Quirk writes that the CDRs deal swiftly with anyone who deviates from the norm, including

> suspected and potential enemies of the government, with presumed counterrevolutionaries, alleged CIA agents, or collaborators, with chronic complainers, with laggards who [stay] home from their jobs and goof-offs who [do] not work hard enough, with homosexuals, and with any writer whose lights [burn] suspiciously or whose typewriter [clacks] late into the night. No citizen [can] feel himself safe from the prying eyes or the suspicious ears of the Committees for the Defense of the Revolution.

The Soviet Trade Deal

Cuban dissidents were not Castro's only critics. The U.S. government strongly condemned many of his new policies. When America made it clear it would not support Cuba with aid, Castro formed an alliance with America's bitter enemy, the Communist Soviet Union.

Castro was wary of aligning himself too closely with the Soviets, since he desperately wanted to make Cuba independent and self-sufficient. He needed Soviet goods and other aid, however. As a result, the Soviets became Cuba's primary trading partner and ally.

In February 1960, the two countries signed a major trade deal. The Russians agreed to buy sugar and other Cuban products in return for oil, steel, iron, and technical assistance. Soviet premier Nikita Khrushchev jubilantly announced, "The Soviet Union is raising its voice and extending a helping hand to the people of Cuba."[70]

In 1963, Castro made his first major visit to the Soviet Union. He was warmly received there. He toured extensively in the vast country and was lavishly entertained in Moscow, including a spectacular parade at the Kremlin in honor of May Day, the international day of celebration for workers.

Castro had always claimed he was not a Communist, but he had read the works of its main theorists: Karl Marx and Vladimir Lenin. As a result, many of his ideas about changing Cuba's social structure were in close harmony with Communist philosophy.

Within a few years of striking his deal with the Soviets, Castro was openly embracing communism. Just after taking power he asserted, "Neither I nor the movement are Communist." Two years later he was saying the opposite: "I shall be a Marxist-Leninist for the rest of my life."[71]

Staying with "the People"

The Soviet trade deal angered American authorities and led to escalating U.S.-Cuban aggression. President Dwight D. Eisenhower cut trade with the island, including shipments of sugar from Cuba and oil deliveries from the United States. Castro retaliated by seizing valuable property belonging to U.S. companies and defiantly telling Eisenhower, "[Y]ou cannot make us bend. . . . You cannot destroy the revolution."[72]

In 1960, Castro traveled to New York City to speak before the United Nations General Assembly. With his flair for publicity, he used the occasion to stage several theatrical moments.

First, Castro rejected the hotel that had been reserved for his group, claiming to be outraged at the price. He led his entourage to the sidewalk outside. Brandishing a hammock before reporters, Castro told them he would sleep in Central Park if necessary.

Announcing he wanted to be with "the people," Castro then checked into the Hotel Theresa, a landmark in Harlem. He had all his meals prepared in the hotel, saying he was afraid of poisoning.

Nikita Khrushchev and Castro (center) embrace during the 1960 United Nations session. Under the two leaders, the Soviet Union and Cuba became close allies.

Khrushchev added to the theatricality of the event. The Soviet leader visited him at the hotel and embraced him before reporters. He remarked that he didn't know if Castro was a Communist, but that he, Khrushchev, had become a *Fidelista.*

Castro's UN speech lasted four and a half hours, the longest in that organization's history. He passionately denounced the United States and twice was reprimanded by the head of the General Assembly, first for claiming that John F. Kennedy and Richard Nixon (then the candidates for the U.S. presidency) lacked brains, and again for calling Kennedy an illiterate, ignorant millionaire who promoted armed revolt in Cuba.

"A COUPLE OF HAIRS"

Not surprisingly, U.S.-Cuban relations continued to deteriorate. America broke off diplomatic relations and stopped all trade except for humanitarian shipments of food and medicine. Castro, in turn, seized all U.S. businesses in Cuba. A military confrontation seemed inevitable.

When the conflict came, it was the result of a secret operation. The Central Intelligence Agency (CIA) had for some time been training and arming anti-Castro Cubans living in the United States for assaults on their homeland. There had already been a handful of small-scale assaults, such as isolated bombings.

For example, Cuban pilots flying U.S. Air Force bombers with Cuban insignia had attacked three Cuban air bases. The CIA hoped that the Cuban insignia would make the world think that Cuban defectors had staged a raid on Castro's air force. The raid was largely unsuccessful, however; Castro had learned of the attack beforehand and was able to move most of his airplanes to safety.

Then, in April 1961 came a large-scale assault on Bahía de Cochinos—the Bay of Pigs. This attack involved a force of about fifteen hundred soldiers, who left by ship from a base in Nicaragua. Nicaraguan president Luis Somoza, no fan of Castro, reportedly told them, "Bring me a couple of hairs from Castro's beard!"[73]

THE BAY OF PIGS

Thanks to his excellent military intelligence, Castro knew the attack was coming. His planes damaged or destroyed most of the fleet from the south. His ground troops, meanwhile, trapped the anti-Castro soldiers on the beach for several days. The invaders dug in and waited for the air support they had understood would be provided. At the last minute, however, Kennedy declined to openly use U.S. forces for this purpose, and Castro's troops easily overwhelmed their compatriots. Although a few members of the assault force escaped, about twelve hundred were captured. Some were executed, but most were ransomed back to the United States in exchange for food and medicine. The final death toll in the operation: 114 invaders and 161 of Castro's soldiers.

The CIA had hoped that the Bay of Pigs attack would inspire the Cuban population to rise up and help overthrow Castro. However, the incident only made Castro more popular. Many Cubans applauded him for defying the powerful United States, which they saw as a bullying aggressor. In honor of the event, Castro erected a billboard on a Bay of Pigs beach reminding visitors that it was the site of the "first imperialist defeat in America."[74]

"THE OTHER FELLOW JUST BLINKED"

Another crisis, the Cuban missile crisis, came in October 1962. Photos from an American spy plane proved the presence in Cuba of twenty long-range Soviet missiles and forty thousand support troops. Khrushchev had ordered that these be placed in Cuba, within range of American targets.

Outraged, Kennedy demanded the withdrawal of the missiles. He imposed a naval blockade—a quarantine zone—five hundred miles from the Cuban coast. The U.S. Navy, Kennedy warned, would fire on any Soviet ship crossing this line.

A tense, thirteen-day standoff followed. It reached an ignition point on October 24, when a Soviet convoy carrying twenty more nuclear warheads neared the quarantine line.

War seemed all but unavoidable. At the last moment, however, Khrushchev ordered the ships to turn around. U.S. Secretary of State Dean Rusk commented, "We have been eyeball to eyeball, and I think the other fellow just blinked."[75]

Over the next week, a settlement was negotiated. Khrushchev agreed to remove his missiles from Cuba. In return, Kennedy promised to never invade Cuba and to remove missiles from Turkey, another political hot spot.

War had been averted, but relations remained extremely hostile. Furthermore, Castro was furious at having been excluded from the negotiations. He was reportedly so angry that he screamed, cursed, and kicked a wall. But, as historian Hugh Thomas wryly notes, Castro never had any real authority in the matter: "Small powers can often begin a world crisis, great powers always end them."[76]

Poison Cigars and More

The Bay of Pigs and the missile crisis were the most public aspects of U.S.-Cuban aggression. During the same period, however, top-secret attempts to kill Castro were also taking place. According to a report released in 1975, at least eight CIA-backed plots occurred between 1960 and 1965. (Castro claims the numbers were in the hundreds.)

Most did not involve straightforward assassination. The CIA knew that Castro presented a difficult target for even the best sniper or bomber. He moved constantly and avoided routine. He also had extremely tight security.

So the American spy agency concocted a number of indirect plans under the code name Operation Mongoose. At least some reportedly involved American crime figures. These gangsters had no love for Castro, who had closed down their Havana gambling casinos.

One plot involved lacing Castro's cigars with poison. Another tried to contaminate his skin-diving suit with tubercle bacilli (tuberculosis). Still another sought to poison Castro's milk shake at one of his favorite restaurants.

Even wilder schemes were proposed but never carried out. One would have embarrassed Castro publicly by dusting his shoes with a powerful chemical that would eventually make all his hair fall out, including his famous beard. Another involved doping Castro's cigars with a hallucinogen during a summit conference, thus sending him on a wild public drug trip. A third suggested rigging a seashell to explode near where Castro was diving.

In September 1963, Castro warned that he might retaliate if these attempts persisted. He remarked, "U.S. leaders should think that if they assist in terrorist plots to eliminate Cuban leaders, they themselves will not be safe."[77] Publicly, however, he appeared unconcerned about the plots. He cheerfully remarked, "I'm not worried. I will not live one day more than the day I am going to die."[78]

Losses

Assassination attempts were one aspect of Castro's public life. He always took great care to keep his very public affairs separate from his private life. He once remarked, "I've always been allergic to

Smoking his trademark cigar, Castro stands atop a podium between two officials. One attempt to assassinate the Cuban leader involved lacing his cigar with poison.

social columns, to publicity about the private lives of public men."[79]

Only a few pieces of information regarding Castro's private life have thus emerged over the years. According to journalist Juan O. Tomayo, "Most Cubans . . . know almost nothing about the personal life of one of the world's most private, even secretive rulers."[80]

As a result, his mother's death in 1963 was the last time anything was reported in the Cuban press about Castro's private life. Even when two of his sisters later fled Cuba, the events went unreported.

Four years after his mother's death, Castro suffered another loss. In 1967, Guevara was killed while on a mission to stir up revolution in Bolivia. This was a personal blow to Castro and, since Guevara had been a major figure in the revolution, it also left a gaping hole in the Cuban government.

However, in a sense Guevara's death had a positive aspect for Castro. It removed his chief rival for the Cuban people's loyalty. Foss notes, "Che's death left Fidel as the only figure who commanded widespread affection."[81]

WORK HABITS

As he bent himself to the difficult task of transforming his country, Castro's work habits displayed the discipline he had learned as a military man. They also bore evidence of his seemingly inexhaustible energy.

Castro routinely put in twenty-hour days, beginning with a detailed briefing of events. He once remarked, "I spend an hour and a half every day reading the wire services, the dispatches from almost all the agencies. I receive them typed, in a folder, with a table of contents. The dispatches are in order, by topic."[82]

The leader generally did not sleep a normal amount, preferring to stay up through most of the night and take short catnaps during the day. His mind was so busy, and his nature so restless, that he could rarely remain still for long. Conchita Fernández, for many years Castro's secretary, recalled that "he would say, 'I'll rest on the couch for three or four hours, and you wake me up at such and such a time,' and ten minutes later he was back in my office to read the correspondence."[83]

Some aspects of Castro's working life remained shadowy. In part this was because he moved constantly, living and working out of many places. The constant movement was partly due to his restless nature. However, it also stemmed from security concerns. Although he professed to be unconcerned about CIA assassination attempts, Castro remained wary and vigilant about attacks from within, as well as from outside, Cuba. As a result, no one but his closest advisers and friends knew exactly what his schedule might be.

He reportedly used several mansions, a hunting estate, and even an entire island for his operations. On rare occasions in the capital, he used Batista's old Presidential Palace. However, Castro's main base of operations was a penthouse suite in what had once been the Havana Hilton.

When not in Havana, Castro traveled nonstop around the country, giving speeches and micromanaging local affairs. Castro was always ready to talk to ordinary Cubans on these journeys. Photographer Roberto Salas recalls, "It might seem hard to believe to some people today, but in the '50s and '60s, the Cuban people had incredible access to Fidel, Che . . . and Raúl. They went everywhere. And anyone could walk up to them and talk to them."[84]

FAMILY

Despite his hectic pace, Castro found time for relaxation. One of Castro's favorite forms of relaxation was hiking in the mountains. A child of the farmlands, he has always loved the countryside. "If it depended on me," he once remarked, "I would always be in the country, in the mountains. I prefer it a thousand times to the city."[85]

Castro also liked skin diving and—still—baseball. For several years after he ascended to power, he occasionally pitched for a team of Sierra Maestra veterans called *Los Barbudos*. Salas recalls that Castro also made surprise appearances on occasion at professional games, where the pro athletes were happy to let him sit in: "He'd just show up at Cerro, the big baseball stadium in Havana, and pitch an inning."[86]

Castro also found time to father more children. One son, Jorge Angel, was born

IMPROMPTU SPEECHES

In these excerpts from a 1985 interview, Castro provides some insights into how he prepares and delivers his famous speeches. The quotes are from Jeffrey M. Elliot and Mervyn M. Dymally's Fidel Castro: Nothing Can Stop the Course of History.

I don't like to repeat speeches. I don't even like to repeat phrases. I find it boring. . . .

Sometimes, [for] appearances where one must use a great deal of facts and figures, then I write the speech. But for some reason, people like it better when the speeches are not written. It seems to me that they like to see the man's struggle—his efforts to elaborate ideas. Sometimes when the audience knows that someone is making a great mental effort to work out his ideas, they can almost guess what's coming, and they follow closely. . . .

The public likes to see the birth of arguments and ideas. This has led me, on certain occasions, to dispense with the written speech and retain a great amount of data—on education, public health, the economy, or other topics—in my head. Sometimes when I speak, I have to keep 80 to 100 facts in my head. . . .

The only advantage in writing out the speech is that the tension disappears and you can sleep easier the night before. You've got it all done—it's just a matter of standing up and reading it. You don't have to give birth to ideas. When you don't have it written, there's the tension of ideas racing in your mind and the pressure of the test. It's like before an exam or a battle. . . .

I have learned that contact with the public—the influence of the public—is the best source of inspiration. Ideas and arguments suddenly take form that didn't occur to you the day before or many days before. When you're in direct contact with the public, nothing is artificial, nothing is abstract. You get better ideas; words are more persuasive, more convincing.

Castro is a seasoned public speaker. Here, he gesticulates during a press conference.

of a mother whose name is unknown. He later had five more sons—Angel, Antonio, Alejandro, Alexis, and Alex—with Dalia Soto del Valle, a former schoolteacher who met Castro during the literacy campaigns of the 1960s. Some reports say she and Castro married, but this has never been officially confirmed.

TROUBLE BREWS

As his policies took shape, *El Líder Máximo* developed slogans and other tools to instill them in everyday Cubans. Schoolchildren, for instance, were taught to honor revolutionary ideals from an early age. They wore military-like uniforms and recited slogans such as "Full Support for the Revolution!" "Fatherland or Death!" or "Study, Work, Rifle."

Castro also appealed to Cuba's national pride to promote the revolution. This was especially necessary as many of his programs began to fail. Castro urged all Cubans to pull together through the difficult first period of the revolution by recognizing that hardships would lead to happiness. Using military discipline as a model, he argued that austerity, personal sacrifice, hard work, and public spirit would lead to national salvation and independence.

Despite these appeals, many of the Cubans who had been loyally supportive in the early days were growing disillusioned. They observed, for one thing, that Castro was tightening his hold on power by quashing dissent and finding ways to keep the people from exercising basic civil liberties.

One of these was the right to vote. Castro kept promising that he would reinstate democratic elections, but they never happened. Another was the right of free speech. Castro maintained his policy of silencing, even imprisoning, dissidents who were critical of his policies.

SHORTAGES

Castro's support was also undermined because many of his campaigns were unpopular, failures, or both. One example was a program in 1968 designed to wipe out free enterprise.

Castro shut down or nationalized thousands of small businesses, even vendors who sold fried-egg sandwiches on streets. He also closed bars, garages, and other gathering places. The idea was to free workers for the fields, but instead the program caused massive disruption of the economy and high prices for goods on the black market.

Dubious reforms like this one, Castro's critics argued, led not to prosperity but to poverty. Almost from the beginning of the revolution there were serious shortages of food and other essentials, and Castro was forced to ration almost all goods. Cubans had trouble finding even ordinary items like lightbulbs, shoelaces, and writing paper.

Furthermore, gaping holes had appeared in Cuba's system of basic services, because so many doctors, lawyers, engineers, and other professionals had left the country. Scores of other problems, such as incompetent central planning, compounded the overall woes. By the end of

A billboard proclaims that the revolution was, is, and always will be a serious movement. As early as the 1960s, however, the shortcomings of Castro's regime became apparent.

the 1960s, Castro's drive to make Cuba self-sufficient was failing.

Cuba simply could not grow enough food. Castro was running up huge debts to the Soviet Union that he could not repay. Urban Cuba's once-vibrant street life was grinding to a halt, and resentment was setting in among the country's normally cheerful and ebullient population. *El Líder Máximo* would spend the next decades trying to keep his dream alive.

Chapter

5 The Firebrand at Home and Abroad

In the wake of his failure to make Cuba self-sufficient, Castro was forced to order the resumption of what the country's climate and soil were best suited for: sugar production. In an attempt to whip up enthusiasm after his previous failures, he designated 1969 the "Year of Decisive Endeavor." (Other years had similar titles: 1963, for instance, had been the "Year of Organization," and 1964 the "Year of the Economy.")

He announced that throughout the next growing season Cuba would grow sugarcane almost exclusively. He also unveiled a wildly ambitious goal: 10 million tons by the end of the next harvest. If successful, he intimated, Cuba could pay off its crushing debt to the Soviets.

However, he warned darkly that it would be difficult. Even one pound less than his goal, Castro declared, would be a defeat, and he warned against sabotage—anyone attempting to undermine the harvest, he announced, would be shot.

FAILURE

Castro extended the harvest season from its normal period of December through February into July 1970. He canceled all holidays, including Christmas and other nonessential activities, so that the country could concentrate on the harvest.

The leader himself set an example by working in the fields for several hours daily, and he ordered millions of workers, students, children, and even foreign guests to do the same. In a speech opening the harvest, he likened the drive to a military attack: "Every worker should act as he would in the face of an enemy attack, should feel like a soldier in a trench with a rifle in his hand."[87]

By the spring of 1970, however, it became clear that Castro's latest scheme was failing. Bad weather, faulty equipment, fire, and blight all played a part in the shortfall. Despite heroic efforts, the harvest fell about 2 million tons short of Castro's goal. Even so, it was a record year; the previous record had been 6 million tons.

Instead of celebrating this new record as an excellent achievement, Castro blamed Cuba's lazy workers and himself. Journalist Georgie Anne Geyer writes, "They were all responsible for the failure, he told his people, but he more than anyone."[88] During this speech, Castro even offered to

A DECADE LATER

Clive Foss, in Fidel Castro, *sums up Cuba ten years after Castro's ascent to power:*

A decade of revolution had produced a new Cuba. Private enterprise was gone, public services and transport were erratic if they existed at all, Havana and other cities were increasingly dirty and shabby. Consumer goods and even many basic foods were impossible to find.

Yet the country was dotted with new hospitals, schools and roads. Slums disappeared as functional new housing sprouted around towns and villages. People might not be able to express themselves freely, but they had access to free education and medical care. Unemployment had virtually disappeared. For every malcontent, there were hundreds still enthusiastic for the revolution, despite the disappointments of the age of experiment.

resign, while the crowd loyally shouted back "No! No!" Few, however, seemed to take the offer seriously.

A DECADE LATER

In addition to the failure of his grand goal, Castro had other things to worry about. A decade into the revolution, Cuba was in many ways in grave condition.

On the one hand, the leader had made some clear improvements in the lives of everyday Cubans. There were dozens of new hospitals, schools, and roads. Slums were disappearing as new housing appeared in various cities and towns. Education and medical care were free to all. Jobs were guaranteed. These guaranteed incomes extended even to creative artists, such as painters, writers, and musicians, as long as they did not create works critical of the government.

However, in many ways things were grave. The Cuban economy was in shambles. Half a million workers had abandoned their regular jobs to work in the sugar fields, so the already weak production system had ground to a virtual halt. Frustrated and disillusioned, many people simply stopped going to work. Jobs may have been guaranteed, but roughly 20 percent of Cuba's workers didn't bother to show up for them.

Meanwhile, private enterprise was almost completely gone. Public services and transportation were erratic, if they existed at all. Consumer goods and even basic food staples were difficult to find. Fear of government reprisals, furthermore, kept citizens from protesting the shortages and other problems.

NEW PLANS

Optimistic and stubborn as ever, Castro pushed his programs ahead. He had not given up his dream of a Cuba made self-sufficient and prosperous through diversified crops. Throughout the 1970s he started or proposed a number of new experiments.

One involved growing new kinds of feed; another involved planting a massive greenbelt of coffee and fruit trees around Havana. Still another scheme was to crossbreed imported cattle with local cattle. Castro promised that the new breed, called F1 (for Fidel), would thrive in tropical conditions and produce record amounts of milk.

As with all his plans, Castro was supremely confident about these and did not like to hear negative comments. When a visiting English scientist pointed out that the laws of genetics doomed the F1 breed to failure, Castro ordered him expelled from Cuba. Despite massive efforts, the F1 plan did indeed fail, as did virtually all of Castro's ambitious agricultural schemes.

Many other plans were floated but never put into action. One of these was Castro's suggestion to replace money with a barter economy. Another involved his confidence that Cuba could produce a cheese that would be superior to any found elsewhere in the world. He also proposed a new Havana airport, even though the existing one was only used for

a few flights a day. Geyer wryly notes, "Ideas like this popped into Castro's mind like mushrooms after the rain."[89]

THE SOVIET EXPERTS

The failure of the grand sugar harvest and his other programs prevented Castro from erasing Cuba's increasingly large debt to the Soviets. Reluctantly, he asked Soviet experts for help in rebuilding the nation's economy. They introduced new policies, such as decentralized decision making and incentives to factory and farm managers. They also found ways to keep Castro's well-intentioned but often disastrous personal meddling, such as his unproven agricultural schemes, to a minimum.

As a result, Cuba's economy recovered to a degree by 1971. Farms and factories became more efficient. Soviet aid increased steadily as well; by the early 1970s, Cuba was receiving about one-third of all the aid and about half the military aid that the Soviets were giving to all of their developing allies.

On the advice of the Soviet experts, Castro also drafted new plans revising his country's political makeup. The main thrust was to make Cuba less dependent politically on the central government in Havana, which had been directing virtually every aspect of life across the country. Local authorities were given greater power in making decisions for their regions.

Castro also drafted a new constitution, formally adopted in 1976, that created a framework for limited elections.

THE CENTER OF ATTENTION IN CHURCH

Castro has rarely acted as though the normal rules of polite society applied to him. He was spoiled as a child, and even as an adult has been known to react petulantly and self-indulgently if things do not go his way.

One example occurred early in Castro's regime. When his sister Emma married a Mexican in 1960, she wanted a large, traditional Roman Catholic ceremony at Havana's largest cathedral. Castro promised to give her away, since their father had already passed away.

Two days before the ceremony, Castro decided that a ceremony in a humble parish church would be more in keeping with the spirit of his revolution. Emma refused to change her plans, however.

In retaliation, Castro did not show up at the cathedral in time. A friend of the groom was hastily recruited to take his place.

El Líder Máximo finally did arrive twenty minutes into the ceremony. He and several other revolutionaries, dressed in army fatigues and boots, clomped noisily into the cathedral and commandeered a front pew. The incident served two purposes for Castro: He made sure that he was the center of attention and he humiliated a sister who had dared to be disobedient.

Individual regions could elect local assemblies, which in turn elected a National Assembly.

This National Assembly was created, in theory, to review and approve new laws. However, its powers were (as they still are) strictly limited, since all of its members belonged to the Cuban Communist Party, the only legal political party in the country. (As of the early 1990s, the party claimed almost 1.5 million members, roughly 10 percent of the population.) Furthermore, the National Assembly meets only a few days a year and reviews legislation that has already been set in motion.

The new constitution also gave Castro new powers and a new title. He became president of the National Assembly's State Council. This consolidated his previous positions of president and prime minister. The leader retained the titles he already had, of commander in chief of the armed forces and secretary general of the Communist Party of Cuba.

ALLIANCES

Despite having to ask for their help, Castro still desperately wanted to keep Cuba as independent from the Soviets as possible. He therefore began a steady round of globe hopping, hoping to create cooperative trade ventures with other countries.

Writer Tad Szulc notes that through this Castro became a "fine practitioner of personal diplomacy."[90]

For a time, Castro was active in the Council for Mutual Economic Assistance (COMECON), a now-defunct alliance of Communist countries. COMECON encouraged its members to produce only what they were best at, with the goal of mutual aid. For example, Czechoslovakia specialized in building streetcars and Hungary in buses.

In Cuba's case, it was sugar. This concentration on producing a single thing was the very situation from which Castro had tried so hard to escape. Nonetheless, Castro believed that mutual aid among the Communist countries was crucial to their survival.

Castro formed a long-lasting alliance with a group known as the Non-Aligned Movement (NAM). This was (and still is) a loose coalition of developing countries in Africa, Asia, and Latin America. In the 1970s, many of these nations had just emerged from, or were still emerging from, colonial rule. What linked them was a mutual unwillingness to align themselves with either of the world's two superpowers.

Castro harvests sugarcane with a machete. Cuba bartered sugar in exchange for other commodities.

EXPORTING THE REVOLUTION

At the same time that he was promoting mutual economic aid, Castro was flexing his military muscle around the world. Always a military man at heart, he supported a number of revolutionary movements by supplying soldiers, doctors, teachers, weapons, and other aid. Among the countries where Castro supported rebel guerrillas were Guinea, Angola, Mozambique, South Africa, Ethiopia, Nicaragua, Namibia, the Republic of the Congo, Colombia, Chile, and Bolivia.

Historian Hugh Thomas comments that Castro's support of such global revolutionary movements was a natural extension of his oversized ambitions. "He was not a man content to confine himself to the small dimension of an island," Thomas writes, "even a large and beautiful one such as Cuba."[91]

The Cuban leader saw Africa as particularly ripe for creating new, revolutionary governments in countries that were just then becoming free of European control. Szulc notes, "Since much of Africa had either been recently decolonized or was peacefully preparing for independence (or fighting for it as liberation movements were doing in the Portuguese colonies), Castro saw an extraordinary potential for Cuban revolutionary influence."[92]

A Personal Touch

Castro justified his support of so many revolutions in Africa by playing up the Afro-Cuban connection. Noting that many Cubans were black or partly black, he stated, "African blood flows freely through our veins. Many of our ancestors came as slaves from Africa."[93]

His most extensive and successful military action was, in fact, in Africa: to rebels in Angola, a former Portuguese colony on the continent's southwest coast. In 1975, a band of Marxists, the Popular Movement for the Liberation of Angola (MPLA), asked Castro for help in repelling a U.S.-backed invasion by the apartheid regime in nearby South Africa.

El Líder Máximo was in his element with this call to arms. He consulted nonstop with troop leaders bound for or already in

Castro converses with Colombian author Gabriel García Márquez during a 2000 fund-raiser. Márquez greatly admired Castro, and the two became close friends.

Angola, and closely followed the details of the fighting.

Castro's friend, the Colombian-born writer Gabriel García Márquez, reports that Castro lent a personal touch whenever troops left Cuba:

> He saw off all the ships, and before each departure he gave a pep talk to the soldiers in the La Cabaña Theater. He personally had picked up the commanders of the battalion of special forces that left in the first flight and had driven them himself in his Soviet jeep to the foot of the plane ramp.[94]

ANGOLA

Castro's military support helped the Angolan rebels to victory. The MPLA was able to send the South African troops into full retreat, and it gained control of most of the country.

Many world leaders, especially those in NAM, saw the victory as a triumph for Castro. He was widely praised, and the organization officially endorsed his actions. NAM further honored Castro by choosing Havana as the site for its next summit meeting.

The success of the Angolan episode overall boosted Castro's popularity around the world, and it was seen in a positive light by many residents of Cuba as well. For them, it took attention away from their country's ongoing economic woes and gave them a sense of pride in a successful job.

Castro was quick to point out that his support in Angola and elsewhere was not just military aid; it included medical, edu-

cational, and technical assistance. Szulc comments that this combination was welcome, since it was coming from a country that was not itself industrialized: "It is a unique formula, accepted by the Angolans, Ethiopians, Nicaraguans, and others in the Third World because it comes from a Third World country."[95]

Although he favored military action, Castro believes that armed revolution is not always the best solution. Sometimes he has advocated democratic elections as a way to create leftist revolution. The most prominent example of this came in 1970 when Marxist leader Salvador Allende, his longtime friend, was elected president in Chile. Allende was the first freely elected socialist leader in Latin America.

Castro praised Allende's ascent to power and urged him to join in forming a community of Latin American nations for mutual support. However, Allende's regime was short-lived. In 1973, the Chilean army, backed by the Central Intelligence Agency, deposed him and installed the dictatorial General Augusto Pinochet as president. The Cuban leader had placed great hope in his future alignment with Allende, but when those dreams were made impossible he resumed his hands-on interest in Africa.

HELPING THE SOVIETS

At the request of the Soviets, Castro sent troops to Ethiopia in 1977 and 1978. Ethiopia, in central East Africa, had just established a Marxist government and was facing a U.S.-backed invasion by neighboring Somalia.

Combined Cuban and Soviet forces successfully kept Somalia out. Many NAM nations, however, believed that Castro was caving in to Soviet demands. They condemned him for this action, which violated NAM's principles of independence.

The Soviets asked Castro for military aid again late in 1979. They wanted his help in a civil war in Afghanistan that was threatening a pro-Soviet government.

Here, Castro was in a difficult position. Afghanistan had been a founding member of NAM; on the other hand, Castro could not afford to refuse the Soviets and risk severing his ties with them.

Castro decided to side with the Soviets by sending thirty thousand Cuban troops to Afghanistan. He was severely criticized by many NAM nations for this. (The Soviets met with serious disapproval as well for their intervention in Afghanistan. Among other repercussions, the United States imposed a grain embargo on the Soviet Union and withdrew its Olympic team from the 1980 Moscow games.)

REVOLUTION IN LATIN AMERICA

Also in 1979, Castro provided significant support for successful battles by two revolutionary movements in Latin America. One was on the Caribbean island of Grenada, where Maurice Bishop, a pro-Cuban socialist, came to power. The other was in Nicaragua. There, the Sandinista National Liberation Front,

also a socialist group, toppled dictatorial president Anastasio Somoza, who had succeeded his more liberal brother Luis in 1967.

The formation of two new socialist states in Latin America boosted Castro's belief in the power of revolution and heightened his reputation among the NAM members. When Castro hosted the group's summit conference that year, he was elected its chairman for the next four years.

That same year, Castro traveled to the United States for the first time in nearly twenty years. His purpose, once again, was to speak before the United Nations.

The last time he had visited, he had been the brash and untested head of a relatively obscure nation. Now he was a true world leader with proven abilities. The

Prime Minister Maurice Bishop of Grenada (left) watches a parade in Havana with Castro. The Cuban leader supported Bishop's 1979 coup to seize control of Grenada.

QUESTIONS FROM AMERICANS

Castro made his second trip to the United States in 1979. At a small dinner reception arranged by television news interviewer Barbara Walters, he was asked a number of questions. Robert E. Quirk, in his book Fidel Castro, *records the response:*

One [guest] asked Castro if he had not lost weight, which pleased him. Another spoke of the World Series. The Cuban president replied that he had hoped to go, but unfortunately he "had other things to do." [Someone] asked if New York had changed since his last visit.

He brightened. "The changes are not in New York but in me." How? "Well," he said, "I am more mature, more responsible, and I have more respect for the United States and for the United Nations. I was a revolutionary then. Now I am a statesman. When I first spoke at the United Nations . . . I did not have a text, and I spoke for five hours. That was wrong. It was not proper. This time I had a text."

He puffed on his cigar and grinned. "The Cubans were nothing then," he said. "It was the United States that made us an important country. They taught us how to defend ourselves."

last time, he had thrown a carefully orchestrated temper tantrum about his hotel, and his hours-long speech before the United Nations had included bitter anti-American abuse. This time, he was on better behavior. There were no grandstanding press conferences, and his speech at the United Nations lasted only two hours. During it, he passionately called on the leaders of the world's richest nations to end hunger, ignorance, disease, and injustice in the developing world.

APEX?

Some Castro observers consider the year 1979 to be the apex of his career. Despite Cuba's floundering economy, its growing population of political prisoners, and its ongoing problem with fleeing refugees, Castro had succeeded in turning his tiny nation into a genuine world force.

His personal popularity in Cuba, meanwhile, was at a high. This was partly because of his successes overseas, but also because he began to abandon the dubious schemes he had tried earlier. Instead, he started to loosen the tight economic controls that had severely restricted everyone not well connected with the Cuban Communist Party or supported by relatives in the United States. For instance, he lifted rationing on some food items. He also let farmers sell surplus produce for profit at "free farmers' markets."

It had been twenty years since Castro took power. He was much the same impassioned, inspiring, and ever-present figure he had been as a dashing revolutionary hero. Physically, he had changed only slightly. His famous curly beard had started to gray, his ever-present cigars were gone, and his clothing had changed from fatigues to a medal-covered officer's uniform.

If 1979 was the pinnacle of Castro's career, 1980 proved to be the beginning of a downward slide. It began with a serious personal blow: Celia Sánchez died of lung cancer. Ever since the Sierra Maestra days, Sánchez had been the leader's closest friend and adviser, maintaining tight control over who had access to him and how he conducted his affairs. Photographer Roberto Salas remarks, "There's no question that she was the most powerful woman in Cuba."[96]

Castro went into a serious depression after her death. The normally outgoing, energetic, and high-spirited leader was withdrawn for months. When he could be persuaded to attend diplomatic receptions or other functions, he was remote and preoccupied. He preferred to spend hours looking at designs for statues to honor Sánchez. For Castro, her death was, writes Geyer, "the one possibility he had never really believed possible."[97]

More Trouble

Sánchez's passing was not Castro's only woe in 1980. Several other events that year proved to be bad fortune for him,

demonstrating that his popular support was beginning to slip.

During the late 1970s, Castro's stubborn anti-American stand had begun to soften slightly. One reason was that Castro hoped to lure Americans—and their dollars—to Cuba. To jump-start the island's nearly defunct tourism industry, he had built several luxurious hotels catering to guests from a variety of countries (and kept them strictly segregated from the Cuban population). Castro wanted to add America to the list.

The U.S. government—now led by President Jimmy Carter, who was relatively open-minded toward Cuba—had reciprocated somewhat. It had dropped the travel ban that had long prevented Americans from visiting. Furthermore, it had been leaning toward lifting the economic sanctions against Castro. However, improved relations between the two countries proved to be short-lived.

Carter served only a single term before being succeeded by Ronald Reagan in 1980. Reagan was deeply conservative and strongly anticommunist. In particular, Reagan was relentlessly anti-Castro. During his two terms in office, the likelihood was slim that relations between the countries might become normal. Historian Clive Foss writes, "For Fidel, the election of Ronald Reagan in 1980 marked the beginning of a decade that culminated in disaster."[98]

Thousands Leave

At the same time, anti-Castro dissension was becoming increasingly open within

President Ronald Reagan poses at his desk in the Oval Office. Reagan was staunchly anticommunist and became Castro's biggest enemy.

Cuba. Symbolic of this dissent were the many antigovernment slogans that appeared on walls around the country; typical of these was "Better exploited under Batista than starving under Castro."[99]

A far more dramatic indication of the Cuban population's unhappiness with Castro was the Mariel boatlift. This was the largest and most visible of the many desperate attempts to flee Cuba.

For years, Castro had been making it progressively more difficult for citizens to get exit visas to leave Cuba legally. In April 1980, a group hoping to find political asylum in Peru crashed a truck through the gates of the Peruvian embassy in Havana.

When the Peruvian ambassador refused to hand the refugees back to the Cuban government, Castro was furious. As punishment, he withdrew all guards from around the South American country's embassy. Then, in an attempt to show that his citizens were free, he grandly announced that any Cubans who wanted to leave could do so. This proved to be a major embarrassment for Castro when ten thousand Cubans crowded into the Peruvian embassy, asking for asylum.

President Carter's term was then just ending. He declared that the United States would welcome Cubans to America. His original proposal was to give sanctuary to about thirty-five hundred Cubans. However,

POLITICAL PRISONERS

In the 1950s, Castro spent roughly three years in prison for speaking out against the ruling government. In spite of this experience, he has regularly imprisoned and even executed those who oppose his own policies.

While no reliable figures are available, some estimates put the number of political prisoners in Cuba in the hundreds or even thousands. Castro insists that Cuba has no political prisoners at all and that all prisoners in Cuba have been jailed on criminal charges.

Organizations that monitor human rights maintain that Cuba's prison conditions are inhumane. Common problems cited include: substandard, dirty, and overcrowded buildings; little or no medical treatment; physical and sexual abuse; poor nourishment; withholding of mail, visitors, fresh air, and exercise; forced "reeducation" sessions; and torture, solitary confinement, and sensory deprivation.

Political prisoners are not necessarily released when their terms are finished, but often languish far longer. Their freedom frequently depends on a personal decision by Castro, who might use the event to gain favor with influential foreign visitors or take advantage of its publicity value.

For example, Vladimiro Roca Antunes, a prominent dissident, was released in May 2002. Roca, who later testified that he had suffered severely while in jail, was released seventy days before the end of his five-year sentence—and just one week before Jimmy Carter became the first U.S. president, former or sitting, to visit Cuba since the revolution.

Castro then made a surprise move, designed to rid his country of thousands of "undesirable" citizens such as criminals and, at the same time, to wreak revenge on the United States for embarrassing him.

MARIEL

Castro announced in *Granma*, the official government newspaper, that all Cubans who so wished were free to go. At the same time, he sent word to the community of Cubans and Cuban Americans in Florida that the small Cuban port of Mariel would be opened. He was sure that a massive evacuation of friends and family would be organized by south Florida residents.

He was right. Tens of thousands of would-be refugees flocked to Mariel and prepared to leave. The Florida-based Cuban community, meanwhile, scrounged thousands of small boats for the Mariel mission. Dangerously overloaded with refugees, these vessels repeatedly shuttled the short distance between Mariel and Florida's southernmost ports.

By the time the boatlift ended in September 1980, more than 120,000 Cubans had fled to America. Twenty-seven died making the crossing, mostly the victims of vessels that sank because of overloading.

Several thousand of the *Marielitos* were criminals, high-risk hospital patients, and mental patients that Castro had released from their institutions and sent to Florida involuntarily. However, the vast majority of the *Marielitos* were people who genuinely wanted to leave the country.

The overall makeup of the Mariel refugees was markedly different from that of the refugees of the 1960s. While the 1960s' refugees had come primarily from the middle and upper classes, most of the *Marielitos* were working class, the sort of Cuban that Castro had once relied on as the foundation of his revolution. The difference dramatically underscored the slackening popular support for Castro's regime.

GRENADA

In the wake of the Mariel affair, Reagan, who had begun his first term in 1981, became even more unbending in his anti-Castro stance. He tightened trade

A Cuban fishing boat overloaded with refugees heads for Key West. More than 120,000 Cubans left the island for America when Castro permitted emigration for several months in 1980.

embargoes, reinstated the ban on U.S. citizens visiting Cuba, and stepped up his broadcasting of anti-Castro radio propaganda. Reagan further announced that any improvement in U.S.-Cuban relations would be dependent on Castro cutting all ties with the Soviets.

Meanwhile, the Cuban economy entered an especially bad slump, thanks to a combination of poor weather, bad planning, debt from Castro's ongoing support of leftist rebels around the world, and fluctuating sugar prices on the global market. By 1983, Castro was actually forced to buy sugar from other countries in order to sell it to the Soviets and thus meet his obligations.

Furthermore, in 1983 a group of hardline Marxists deposed and killed Castro's ally Maurice Bishop, Grenada's socialist leader. Reagan, worried about the presence of another anti-American government in the Caribbean, authorized an invasion of the tiny island by U.S. troops.

A few hundred Cuban military advisers and construction workers were on Grenada at the time. Castro ordered them to fight to the last man. U.S. soldiers tried to avoid contact with the Cubans, but there was conflict nonetheless. The tiny

A Havana street banner proclaims "Socialism or Death!" Castro relied on the power of such slogans to sustain support for his government during times of economic hardship.

Cuban force was overwhelmed; twenty-four Cubans were killed and fifty-nine were wounded. A frustrated Castro, rather than praising the survivors, reprimanded and demoted them for not obeying his orders to fight to the death.

THIRD WORLD DEBT

Throughout the 1980s, Castro remained on the world stage by vigorously promoting an issue close to his heart: the cancellation of Third World debt. All of the developing nations, he argued, were crushed under debts they could not repay.

Cuba, of course, was no exception. It has been estimated that at one point the Soviet Union was spending about $12 million a day on Cuba. At its highest point, Cuba's debt to the larger nation totaled more than $18 billion.

Castro argued that if the world's industrialized nations cut their weapons budgets by only 12 percent, enough money would be freed to cancel all Third World debt and reduce the gap in living standards significantly. He further argued that trying to force developing countries to pay this debt was an impossible task.

The pressure to pay would cause deadly riots, Castro predicted, because the people who would suffer the most were ordinary citizens. He remarked, "You would practically have to kill the people to force them to make the sacrifices required to pay that debt. Any democratic process that tries to impose those restrictions and sacrifices by force will be destroyed."[100]

At home, meanwhile, Castro continued to expound on his philosophy of personal sacrifice. He appealed to all Cubans to practice austerity and to give up the desire for luxuries. This, he said, was the only way that his ideals for Cuba could be fulfilled.

A new patriotic slogan appeared everywhere in the country in honor of the thirtieth anniversary of the revolution: *Socialismo o muerte!* (Socialism or death!) Such slogans, and the loyalty they inspired, would carry Castro into the 1990s.

6 Hard Times

Castro was always wary of both his alliance with the Soviet Union and the threat posed by his neighbor, America. Referring to the respective symbols for the United States and the Soviet Union, Castro once remarked, "I don't know which is more dangerous for the Cuban revolution—the eagle in front of us or the bear we have at our backs."[101]

Despite his wariness, however, Castro remained heavily dependent on the Soviet Union throughout the 1980s to subsidize his country. Now, at the beginning of the 1990s, it appeared that this support was coming to an end. Although as late as 1984 Castro was still calling the Soviet Union "the fundamental pillar of our present and future," the pillar was about to crumble.[102]

ENTER GORBACHEV

In 1985, Mikhail Gorbachev had come to power in the Soviet Union, ascending to the role of secretary general of the Soviet Communist Party. Gorbachev was a reform politician. Faced with a weak economy, inefficient bureaucracy, and widespread discontent, he launched a series of wide-ranging political reforms throughout his government and country.

Chief among these were programs that came under the general headings of glasnost (openness toward other countries) and perestroika (restructuring social, political, and economic life). They brought his government away from hard-line communism and closer to a capitalist, free-market economy. They also introduced dramatic changes in the way the Soviet Union dealt with its allies and enemies.

Castro was deeply opposed to the changes Gorbachev introduced. He remained defiant in the face of the Soviet programs and refused to introduce similar reforms in his own country. He did not, for instance, introduce democratic elections, allow open criticism of his government, or express any desire for friendship with America.

By 1988, Castro was openly criticizing Gorbachev. He predicted that too much reform would destroy socialism—a prediction that would soon prove true in the case of the Soviet Union. One reason he was critical of Gorbachev was that the Soviet reformer's sweeping new policies included severe limitations on Soviet aid to other countries. Castro, of course, was worried about what would happen to Cuba if Gorbachev withdrew aid.

THE SOVIET UNION COLLAPSES

Castro's concerns were well founded. In 1989, Gorbachev announced that the Soviet Union would no longer support Cuba with economic subsidies, which by now amounted to an estimated $6 billion annually. He announced that the Soviets would also withdraw their military and technical aid from the country.

Gorbachev walks alongside Castro during a 1989 visit to Cuba. Gorbachev ended Soviet subsidies to the island state.

Any future trade with Cuba, Gorbachev decreed, would have to be based on profitability, not politics. The future of military aid to the island, furthermore, would depend on his newly improved and much friendlier relationship with the United States. Since the two superpowers were becoming much less hostile toward each other, the likelihood of a continued Soviet military presence in Cuba seemed unlikely.

In April 1989, just as Cuba's subsidies were ending, the Soviet leader visited Havana and signed a twenty-five-year friendship treaty with Castro. However, this was little more than a gesture; the former relationship no longer existed, and both men knew it.

As Castro had predicted, reform was leading to the collapse of the Soviet Union. Gorbachev's reforms had led to a wave of freedom movements in the republics that formed the Soviet Union. As these members of the Soviet bloc asserted themselves, they broke away into independent countries, often bolstering their fights with a renewed sense of ethnic identity. The old union began to dissolve.

A "SPECIAL PERIOD"

The Soviet Union's collapse, when it came in 1990–1991, dealt a severe blow to Castro. Soviet aid to Cuba, in the form of food and other supplies, dropped to almost nothing.

As a result, daily life across the island became even grimmer than it had been. New rounds of rationing made it nearly

Habañeros *wait several hours in line to obtain bread from a bakery. After the collapse of the Soviet Union, food shortages became common in Cuba.*

impossible to find even ordinary items like tobacco, soap, and cooking oil. Cubans had to line up for hours for basic food items such as sugar and flour, or spend hours scavenging for them on the black market; even then, they were not always successful in getting them.

It was in this extremely challenging economic environment that "dollar stores" appeared. These were special stores that accepted only hard currency—that is, foreign currencies, such as American dollars, that were more valuable than the Cuban peso.

More goods were available to tourists in the dollar stores than could be found in the ration shops used by Cubans. As a re-

sult, people desperately looked for ways to acquire dollars and other hard currency. Clive Foss notes, "The obvious source was tourists. Doctors abandoned their surgeries to drive taxis, engineers became waiters, and thousands of women turned to prostitution."[103]

Factories and farms, meanwhile, were crippled by severe shortages of oil, gas, and spare parts. Cuba's all-important sugar harvest was especially threatened by a lack of spare parts and fuel for the harvesting machinery that farms needed.

Desperate to offset these hardships, Castro announced the formation of a "Special Period in Peacetime." He called on the Cuban people, once again, to tighten their

THE GOOD AND THE BAD

For many visitors, the Cuba of the 1990s seemed to be in a time warp. Antique American cars from Batista's days cruised along largely empty streets. The urban fabric of Havana and other cities was intact though crowded and dilapidated. The sight of a building that had crumbled on to the street or was precariously held up by beams was not unusual.

On the other hand, the cities were not disfigured by freeways, parking lots, fast food stores or shopping malls, though increasing prosperity at the end of the decade gradually began to change that. Yet tourists rarely saw the vast rings of functional housing that the revolution had built around the cities, or the thousands of new schools, or had occasion to visit the doctors who could be found in any neighbourhood.

Despite everything, Castro had managed to preserve the revolution and keep the country going. For the first time in its history, Cuba was truly independent. The price had been high, but for those who still believed in the revolution, it might have seemed justified. The rest could only wait.

A parade of antique American cars makes its way along a Havana street.

belts and prepare for another round of personal sacrifices. He also authorized a series of widespread emergency measures during the "special period."

All noncritical factories and services were closed. Thousands of city dwellers were ordered to the countryside to work on farms, in an attempt to increase sugar production.

To offset the shortage of spare parts and fuel, Castro directed that horses and oxen were to be used in the countryside instead of tractors. In the cities, Castro imported thousands of bicycles from China to replace sidelined buses and taxis.

Castro warned the nation, in speech after speech, about a dire prospect he saw in the future. He called it "Zero Option"— the inevitable point at which support from the Soviets would completely stop. This possibility was brought into sharp focus early in 1991, when a Soviet ship carrying grain and flour did not arrive in Cuba as hoped. Because of the failure of this single shipment, Castro was forced to cut bread rations and sharply raise the price of other foodstuffs.

ZERO OPTION

That summer, Zero Option finally came to pass. The last of the Soviet troops withdrew from Cuba and the long-standing flow of aid trickled to a halt.

Already barely able to feed itself, the Cuban population began to suffer worse than ever. By 1992, the average daily calorie intake of the nation was down to nine hundred, far below any recognized level for healthy living (two thousand calories per day is a frequently used standard). Meanwhile, the country's economy was crumbling; exports fell by 60 percent and imports by 70 percent.

Nonetheless, Castro remained defiant. He was not willing to make changes to the programs he had in place, and he stubbornly vowed to see the current crisis through. Remaining, as always, enthusiastic about Cuba's prospects for the future, he also tried to put the situation in the best light possible. He hoped to make people realize that the "special period" was actually a positive development that would result in a stronger Cuba.

For instance, he was enthusiastic about the possibilities of alternative sources of energy, hoping to end Cuba's dependence on foreign oil. At one point, he proposed that Cuba abandon mechanical power completely and embrace animal power.

He suggested that the use of animals over tractors was actually preferable for work in the sugarcane fields. In wet weather, he explained, oxen were far more useful than tractors, because they did not break down and could slog through mud better. He enthused, "Could anything be more healthy? . . . Someday we might be thankful for this special situation. We are going back to the ox, the noble ox."[104]

"I NEED A CANDLE"

Despite Castro's enthusiasm, conditions grew worse, and his political base within Cuba dwindled further. Outright criticism and even rebellion appeared more and more frequently. Castro retaliated by continuing to suppress this public opposition as much as possible. One aspect of this was the formation of "Rapid Response Brigades."

These groups augmented the Committees for the Defense of the Revolution, the neighborhood groups of spies that Castro had established decades earlier. The new "brigades" were essentially nothing more than violent gangs of loyal *Fidelistas.* They had orders to break up public protests and harass anyone who dared to speak out against the government.

At the same time, Castro did his best to revive Cuba's economy. One method he used was to renew efforts to attract foreign tourists to Cuba's legendary beaches. He did this by establishing new policies such as one creating special zones around Cuba's best beaches and attractions. In these special zones, foreigners could

SCANDAL

During the late 1980s, Castro personally involved himself in the biggest state trial since he had taken power. Known simply as Judicial Case No. 1, the incident involved accusations of treason and corruption on the part of some of Castro's closest associates.

The trial served two useful purposes for Castro. It riveted the nation's attention, dominating the news for months and creating a welcome diversion from Cuba's worsening troubles. It also allowed Castro to rid himself of a number of top-echelon colleagues who had become troublesome.

At the heart of the scandal was one of the country's most prominent figures, General Arnaldo Ochoa. Ochoa was Cuba's most successful general, a hero of the Bay of Pigs who later commanded Cuban forces in Angola and Ethiopia.

However, Ochoa had been openly critical of Castro's tactics in Angola, and had also found fault with the leader's attitude toward returning Cuban veterans. Furious, Castro had Ochoa arrested—despite a lack of evidence—on charges of smuggling gold and ivory out of Angola and of conspiring to deal drugs in Panama.

Two other high-ranking politicians, brothers called the de la Guardia twins, were also arrested, along with several other lower-ranking officials. The de la Guardias and the lower-ranking officials were mostly guilty, at least of smuggling, while Ochoa was almost certainly not. However, in the public eye Ochoa was lumped together with the guilty parties.

A televised court martial, over which Castro personally presided, handed out death sentences to Ochoa, the de la Guardias, and several others. They were executed by firing squad, and Castro filled their places with politicians more sympathetic to his ideas.

freely spend money in the dollar stores on items not available to ordinary Cubans.

Castro's measures were widely resented by his constituents. While some continued to support their longtime leader, an increasing number did not. As the economic situation worsened, with the average Cuban barely able to feed him- or herself, even the most loyal *Fidelistas* could not avoid a sense of desperation. One man, a revolutionary and a veteran of the Sierra Maestra campaign, summed up the feelings of many when he lamented, "Hope? I need a candle to look for hope here. There's no future in Cuba."[105]

A NEW GENERATION OF REFUGEES

People had been abandoning their homes, and often families, in Cuba since the early days of Castro's regime. Even after the Mariel boatlift in 1980, the ranks of the discontented grew. During the 1990s, increasing numbers of people tried to leave. In 1994, a Cuban military ship sank a boatload of escaping refugees. Forty-one people drowned, including twenty-one women and children.

Stung by international criticism of this incident, that same year Castro once again announced an open migration policy. More than thirty thousand Cubans attempted to cross the Straits of Florida in the months afterward, many of them using the famous *balsas*, homemade rafts, or even large inner tubes. Reliable statistics are impossible to come by, but published reports suggest that at least a thousand *balseros* did not survive the dangerous crossing during this wave of migration.

Cuban refugees cross the Straits of Florida on a homemade raft with an outboard motor. Many still lose their lives attempting this dangerous crossing.

Many of these refugees were part of a younger generation of Cubans. This generation had grown up entirely under the revolution. They had no memories of Fulgencio Batista, no idea how corrupt and repressive his government had been. They had no sense (other than their parents' and grandparents' stories) of how terrible life had been for most Cubans before Castro took over.

Furthermore, they rarely appreciated the progress Castro had made. They did not remember the overwhelming sense of hope he had once brought to an oppressed Cuba. They took for granted the benefits of socialism, such as guaranteed jobs, subsidized housing, and universal, free medical care and education. They were also less willing to endure hardships than their parents in the name of patriotism.

Instead, they generally saw Castro as an outmoded leader, hopelessly out of touch. This younger generation also craved the political freedom and high standard of living they knew existed elsewhere. Georgie Anne Geyer writes that they were "the children of American videos, of rock music, of a constant yearning for the world outside."[106]

LETTING THE CHURCH IN

The discontent of many notwithstanding, Castro continued to pursue most of his revolutionary policies and remained steadfastly opposed to open dissent. Yet, he was changing in one way. For reasons that are not entirely clear, during this period he was slowly easing his decades-long ban on religion.

Specifically, he was letting go of some of the restrictions he had imposed on the Catholic Church. This had begun in 1988, when Castro met with John Cardinal O'Connor, the archbishop of New York. The meeting signaled a gradual thaw.

In 1991, Castro allowed Catholics, for the first time, to join the Cuban Communist Party. Gradually, he made other changes as well. He withdrew security agents from Cuban churches, allowed public outdoor masses to be held, and allocated money for the restoration of Cuba's many beautiful church buildings, which had grown dilapidated through neglect.

In 1996, a major step forward was taken when Castro traveled to Rome and visited Pope John Paul II at the Vatican. During the visit, the Cuban leader invited the pope to visit Cuba. The following year, in 1997, Christmas was openly celebrated in Cuba for the first time in more than thirty years.

When the pope paid a visit to Cuba in 1998, Castro permitted the staging of four huge open-air masses. He provided media coverage for these events and arranged for special public transportation, so that faithful Catholics in far-flung regions of Cuba could attend them.

Appearing in Cuba before cheering crowds of ecstatic Catholics, the pope delivered a number of messages. He praised the people's faith but also counseled Cuban Catholics to take more responsibility for change within their country.

John Paul was strongly critical of both the United States and Cuba. He characterized the U.S. trade embargo as inhumane.

However, he also spoke out against Castro for curbing freedom for Cuban citizens and continuing to hold political prisoners. Shortly afterward, Castro freed about three hundred prisoners, about seventy of whom had been held on political charges.

CONTINUED TENSION WITH THE UNITED STATES

Not all of Castro's problems were within the boundaries of Cuba. In particular, his ongoing conflicts with America worsened, especially over the immigration question.

The problem was resolved to a degree when he and Reagan reached a formal agreement that allowed a minimum of twenty thousand legal immigrants per year from Cuba to the United States. However, his overall relations remained hostile with the American president and his successor, George H.W. Bush.

Bush, like Reagan, took a hard-line anti-Castro stand. For instance, he widened America's trade sanctions to include a ban on trade with Cuba by foreign subsidiaries of U.S. companies. This and other measures effectively stopped all goods, including food and medicine, from being imported into Cuba from any U.S. sources.

Furthermore, Bush said that the United States would not consider easing these sanctions unless Castro made significant concessions. Among these were requirements that Cuba hold free, democratic, internationally supervised elections; adopt a free-market economy; and cut the size of its armed forces.

In vote after vote, the UN General Assembly strongly recommended that the

President Bill Clinton delivers a speech. He imposed stringent legislation restricting American relations with Cuba.

United States end this long-standing embargo against Cuba. However, in 1996 Bush's successor, Bill Clinton, signed even more stringent legislation. This law, the Helms-Burton Act, imposed penalties on foreign companies doing business in Cuba, permitted U.S. citizens to sue foreign investors who made use of American-owned property seized by Cuba, and denied entry into the United States to such foreign investors.

This act was drafted in the wake of an aggressive military action by Castro. He had directed Cuban fighter jets to shoot down two unarmed, U.S.-registered aircraft. These airplanes had been piloted by members of *Los Hermanos al Rescate* (Brothers to the Rescue), a relief organization dedicated to spotting and, if possible, rescuing Cuban refugees in danger of not surviving the difficult passage.

Despite the stranglehold that America's trade and travel restrictions continued to have on his country, Castro remained defiant toward the United States. He often repeated a statement, which he had made many times in various forms over the years: "We have no contact with the U.S. and we don't want any."[107]

ISOLATED

Castro's problems during the 1990s extended to other countries besides the United States. He was, by this time, one of a decreasing number of dictators around the world, thanks in large part to a new, global wave of democratic movements.

Sometimes, these movements toward democracy replaced Castro's friends and allies. Two such incidents came late in 1989, when American troops invaded Panama, deposed General Manuel Noriega, and brought the dictator to Miami for trial on drug trafficking charges. Shortly afterward, another group of Latin American leaders allied closely with Castro, the Sandinistas in Nicaragua, suffered a huge defeat in nationwide elections.

Because he held to his policies, including those that entailed human rights violations and economic hardship for his

PUBLIC MAN

In Jeffrey M. Elliot and Mervyn M. Dymally's Fidel Castro: Nothing Can Stop the Course of History, *the Cuban leader comments on the problems of his public life:*

I go anywhere. I visit the universities and other schools. I meet with many people, both Cubans and foreigners, and my work becomes a natural thing. But sometimes crowds gather where I go.

How long since I last ate at a restaurant? Why? A new Chinese restaurant recently opened in Old Havana, which is being restored. It's small and cozy, in an old building. For some time, I've wanted to go to the restaurant. But if I go, a crowd may gather. I can't conceive of sitting there quietly, eating on the second floor, while a large crowd of people stand in the street, waiting to see me. Still, these are minor inconveniences, which go with the job. . . .

I've never had that fishbowl feeling of being viewed through a microscope, or living in an ivory tower. I've really not felt it.

people, Castro became increasingly isolated from other world leaders, many of whom had once been allies. Overall, fewer statesmen were willing to join Castro in openly defying the United States, which in the wake of the Soviet collapse had become the world's only superpower.

Several national leaders who had been sympathetic to Castro urged him to move quickly toward democracy. They argued that he would have to change soon if he hoped to survive.

INSULTED IN SPAIN

The steep drop in Castro's support among world leaders—as well as his weakening popularity with everyday people around the world—was graphically illustrated during his first major trip to Spain, in the summer of 1992. (He had visited there briefly once before, in the 1980s.)

Castro traveled to Madrid to take part in a summit conference of Spanish-speaking countries. The trip was one of Castro's continuing attempts to establish friendly relations in Latin America and Europe.

The journey to his father's homeland should have been a personal triumph for Castro. "Fidel finally traveled to his father's Spain for a major trip, one that had been put off for many years," Geyer writes. "He fully expected the odyssey to be a magnificent, stirring, triumphal moment in his lifetime."[108]

Instead, Castro got a notably chilly reception. Crowds of protesters and picketers booed him. Spain's most influential newspaper called him a "dying star." And Felipe Gonzalez, the country's socialist prime minister and once a political ally, publicly snubbed him.

SIGNS OF A THAW

Despite such incidents indicating Castro's increasing isolation, there have been occasional signs that the U.S.-Cuban standoff may ease slightly. *Beisbol*, the sports passion of all Cuba and especially of Castro, was the catalyst for one such display, when a pair of exhibition baseball games took place between American and Cuban teams.

In 1999, the Baltimore Orioles played the Cuban All-Stars in Havana. It was the first appearance by a major league club in Havana in forty years. Castro appeared on the field before the game, waving to the crowd of fifty thousand and shaking the hands of all the players. The Orioles won that first matchup 3–2. However, the next day in Baltimore the Cuban team trounced the Orioles 12–6.

More direct forms of diplomacy have traditionally come in terms of trade agreements, and these have slowly opened. In 2000, the United States began easing to a degree its economic restrictions on Cuba. Several bulk shipments of items such as apples, onions, corn, rice, and wheat were delivered to the island.

The first shipments of food from the United States to Cuba in almost forty years were allowed in 1992, as a humanitarian gesture following a devastating hurricane. The first sale (since the onset of

Before the 1999 game in Havana, the Baltimore Orioles and the Cuban national team stand at attention during the American and Cuban national anthems.

trade restrictions) of brand-name American food directly to Cuba occurred in 2002. That year, an Indianapolis supermarket chain delivered a shipment to Cuba of butter, margarine, and cereal.

AMID POSITIVE SIGNS, SOME TROUBLING ALLEGATIONS

There have been several other signs in recent years that the United States and Cuba may be regarding each other more favorably. For instance, in 2001 Castro was nominated for the Nobel Peace Prize for his work in aiding other developing nations. Although the Nobel Prize is awarded in Sweden, its prestige and fame helped raise Americans' awareness of some of Castro's achievements.

The following year, Jimmy Carter became the first sitting or former president to visit Cuba since the revolution began. Both Carter and Castro declared the visit a success. Other politicians and organizations have made concerted efforts in recent times to open cultural, political, and trade doors.

Despite such efforts, however, the United States and Cuba remain mostly hostile toward one another. In 2002, the week before Carter's visit, Clinton's successor as president, George W. Bush, denounced Castro. Bush claimed that the Cuban leader was developing biological weapons and harboring terrorists, such as members of the Irish Republican Army and the Basque separatist movement.

Bush further characterized Cuba as part of an "axis of evil" that includes Iraq, Iran, North Korea, Libya, and Syria. Castro denied Bush's allegations, challenging the United States to present proof. He pointed out that he had denounced terrorism following the September 11, 2001, attacks on America, expressing solidarity with the American people and offering to cooperate to defeat terrorism.

NEXT CHRISTMAS IN HAVANA?

For decades, many observers have predicted Castro's imminent fall. They have felt that in recent years, with his support at home crumbling and his peers around the world shunning him, he could not last much longer. Every year, Cuban Americans in Miami and elsewhere have waited for the Castro regime to topple, and "next Christmas in Havana" have become common bywords.

However, Castro has defied these predictions. He has stayed in power year after year, deflecting all potential usurpers, still struggling to create his dream of a socialist state in Cuba.

In so doing, he has continued to maintain what is essentially a police state, with himself as the absolute leader. Castro emphatically denies being a dictator; however, he continues to hold all the highest offices and to control virtually all aspects of Cuban life. Open opposition to the government is not allowed. No official figures telling how many political prisoners are being held in Cuba are available, either to ordinary Cubans or to the international community.

The Cuban Communist Party, meanwhile, still controls the country's elections. The National Assembly sits only a few days a year to review legislation that has already been set in motion. These laws all stem from, or at least are approved by, Castro himself. Foss writes, "What he proposed in a speech on television [is] soon made into law."[109]

STILL SUPPORT

Despite ongoing and persistent criticism, Castro retains some support, especially among older Cubans. These *Fidelistas* fear the replacement of their leader with a government made up of men and women who abandoned their country when times were hard. They worry that "Americanized" Cubans would, at best, be disadvantageous to Castro loyalists and, at worst, could bring back the corruption and injustice of the Batista era.

Meanwhile, they point to Castro's many positive achievements. They admire his decades of struggle to stay free of U.S. influence. They appreciate the Cuban system of guaranteed jobs and fear the example of Eastern Europe, where as much as 40 percent of the population became unemployed following the collapse of the Communist regimes.

They also appreciate Castro's system of subsidized housing and free education. They argue, as well, that Castro has achieved in Cuba the highest literacy rate in the Third World.

Furthermore, they argue, Castro has created an impressive free health care system. As a result of this system, Cuba has the longest average life span—seventy-six years—in the developing world, and its infant death rate has fallen to the point where it rivals those of even the wealthiest developed nations.

With help from these loyal *Fidelistas*, and despite all the odds, Castro continues to hold on to his power into the new millennium. How long that hold will last, and what shape it may take, is open to speculation.

Holding On

Castro is still, by any measure, the most public figure in Cuba. *El Líder Máximo* remains a major presence in the daily lives of every Cuban: His image is ubiquitous on television, his voice is a constant on the radio, and his opinions are freely quoted in the newspapers. He is still fond of goading his old enemy the United States whenever possible, as when the return to Cuba of Elián González, a five-year-old refugee, became a major news story in 1999–2000.

The face and the voice have, of course, changed since the heady days of the revolution. Castro's beard has become completely gray, and there are deep lines in his face. When he delivers one of his epic speeches, the fire of the early days is gone. Some observers say he is in poor health—a dramatic change from the days when his mental energy and physical strength were legendary.

STEPPING DOWN?

The leader credits a positive outlook, as well as such pastimes as skin diving and playing baseball, for keeping him in good humor and health. He once commented to an interviewer,

> [I]f I really didn't have a sense of humor, if I didn't joke with others and even with myself, if I weren't able to let go, I wouldn't have been able to handle the job. I also ask myself the same questions. How's my blood pressure? How's my heart doing? How have I been able to stand it for so many years?[110]

However, as he edges closer to eighty, even some faithful *Fidelistas* wonder if it is time for Castro to step down. He could, they suggest, possibly be succeeded by Raúl, the hard-line Marxist who has always remained quietly in his brother's shadow.

Castro has repeatedly said that he will not continue to hold power if he does not have the support of the Cuban population. He once remarked, "[I]f one day the revolution did not have the support of the overwhelming majority of the people, it could not endure. This revolution cannot be sustained in power by force."[111] Elsewhere, he has commented, "If tomorrow I were to resign all my functions, there'd

In 1985, Castro commented on his own aging and health in this passage from Jeffrey M. Elliot and Mervyn M. Dymally's Fidel Castro: Nothing Can Stop the Course of History:

The more the years go by, the less I worry about death and old age. Isn't that curious? What could have contributed to this? I would say that twenty years ago, I thought I needed a lot of time to fulfill a mission, to complete a task. As time passes, you start to get the feeling that a large part of the task that was your lot in life has already been fulfilled and that what you have accomplished lives on. Then you are less anxious about health, age, and death.

have to be a truly convincing reason for the people to understand it."[112]

CASTRO AT HOME

Throughout the decades, Castro has apparently lived up to his personal credo of austerity and simple living. Unlike many absolute dictators who abuse their power, Castro has never indulged in fancy cars, lavish houses, or other trappings of power and wealth. Until he gave them up, good Cuban cigars were among his few indulgences.

Castro continues to live simply today. He and his longtime partner (and perhaps wife) Dalia Soto del Valle live in a two-house compound in Havana. Raúl Castro lives only a few blocks away.

Not much is known about the details of Castro's house. It has been reported that the living room is simply furnished with plain furniture and Cuban crafts. The only luxury apparent to visitors is a big-screen

television. Castro uses this to satisfy his passion for foreign news and sports, as well as to watch videos recorded by his intelligence services.

Outside, there are tennis and basketball courts. Trees block the compound from curious onlookers and electronic fences detect intruders. The streets around the home are all one-way, pointed away from the house. Only official cars are allowed to drive the wrong way to reach the house.

The Castro brothers used to use several other houses around the island as residences during vacations or official visits to the provinces. After Cuba's plunge into economic crisis in 1991, however, these accommodations began to see use as tourist lodgings.

PRIVATE LIFE

Despite his very public face, Castro has remained throughout his long reign of power fanatically private and reclusive about his personal life. Most Cubans know almost nothing about their leader's personal life or his family, since the Cuban media is strictly forbidden from reporting on it.

Alina Fernandez, Castro's only daughter, rebelled for years against her father's revolutionary ideals and his principles of austerity and sacrifice. After years of trying to escape Cuba, she finally succeeded in 1993. Settling in Spain, she wrote a scathingly negative book about her father. She has since moved to Miami and continues to be highly critical of her father in public.

Fidelito is the only one of Castro's children who has been regularly mentioned in Cuban media. This was especially true from 1980 to 1992, when he was the executive secretary of the Cuban Atomic Energy Commission. Little is known about his more recent activities, although it has been reported that he is a consultant for the Ministry of Basic Industries and has divorced his Russian wife to remarry a Cuban.

Castro's other sons hold relatively obscure jobs, such as computer programming. They do not participate in politics, whether for lack of interest or because they are not allowed to, and so are unlikely to succeed *El Jefe.* All but the youngest live away from their parents' home. Most, reportedly, are married and have children of their own, making Castro a grandfather many times over.

No one in Cuba is allowed to live lavishly, and this includes the Castro family. Castro's sons, for instance, are under strict

Fidel Castro emphasizes a point during a celebration of the thirtieth anniversary of the revolution. As Castro grows older, questions concerning the future of Cuba have begun to surface.

"THE DAYS OF ITS DESTRUCTION"

Foreign correspondent Georgie Anne Geyer is no fan of Castro or his policies. Her remarks, excerpted from her book Guerrilla Prince: The Untold Story of Fidel Castro, *perhaps represent the feelings of many anti-Castro observers.*

He had an enormous effect on the twentieth century. The numbers of people who owed their deaths to Fidel Castro are difficult to establish, his influence and power were so often so amorphous, [but] one has to come to the conclusion that he is personally responsible for the deaths of hundreds of thousands of persons.

He is also supremely responsible for drawing out poisoned situations into endless conflicts—without his involvement, these conflicts would have ended far more quickly and far more decisively, with immeasurably far less suffering. In the end, he also killed culture; he killed a Cuba that, left alone and with a real reform, would have evolved into a developed and reasonably just nation in the time that he ruled over the days of its destruction. In the end, he left only silence and emptiness, fear and hatred, obsession and exhaustion.

---

orders to avoid conspicuous behavior. "They don't dress any better than anyone else," according to Fernandez. "On the contrary, they are required to at least project an image of austerity for the rest of the Cubans."[113]

CUBA WITHOUT FIDEL

Castro has always excited violent passions, both pro and con. The ways in which he will be regarded by future generations will no doubt be equally varied. Historian Clive Foss notes, "History may view him as a revolutionary hero who spread the idea of liberation through the world or as an ossified despot who has transformed one of the richest countries of Latin America into one of the poorest. Most likely, he combines the elements of both."[114]

The questions of how the revolution will play itself out without Castro and of what will happen to a Cuba that has been controlled so thoroughly by one man for so long are fascinating ones. Journalist Georgie Anne Geyer asks, "What would happen 'after Fidel'? What could happen after Fidel? And, by far the most compelling question: Can you have *Fidelismo* without Fidel?"[115]

What the future holds for Castro is, of course, unknown. Such questions can only be answered after the twin dramas—the intertwined destinies of Cuba and Fidel Castro—have played themselves out.

Notes

Introduction: El Jefe

1. Jon Lee Anderson, foreword to *Fidel's Cuba: A Revolution in Pictures,* by Osvaldo Salas and Roberto Salas. New York: Thunder's Mouth Press, 1998, p. 6.

2. Tad Szulc, *Fidel: A Critical Portrait.* New York: Morrow, 1986, p. 23.

3. Quoted in Lee Lockwood, *Castro's Cuba, Cuba's Fidel.* New York: Macmillan, 1967, p. 178.

Chapter 1: Young Fidel

4. Quoted in Frei Betto, ed., *Fidel and Religion: Castro Talks on Revolution and Religion with Frei Betto.* New York: Simon and Schuster, 1987, p. 144.

5. Robert E. Quirk, *Fidel Castro.* New York: Norton, 1993, p. 9.

6. Quoted in Betto, *Fidel and Religion,* p. 91.

7. Quoted in Betto, *Fidel and Religion,* p. 100.

8. Quirk, *Fidel Castro,* p. 3.

9. Quoted in Georgie Anne Geyer, *Guerrilla Prince: The Untold Story of Fidel Castro.* Kansas City, MO: Andrews and McMeel, 2001, p. 22.

10. Quoted in Betto, *Fidel and Religion,* p. 144.

11. Quoted in Szulc, *Fidel,* p. 109.

12. Quoted in Betto, *Fidel and Religion,* p. 113.

13. Quoted in Szulc, *Fidel,* p. 115.

14. Quoted in Deborah Shnookal and Pedro Álvarez Tabío, eds., *Fidel: My Early Years.* Melbourne, Australia: Ocean Press, 1998, p. 77.

15. Quoted in Geyer, *Guerrilla Prince,* p. 32.

16. Quoted in Shnookal and Tabío, *Fidel,* p. 73.

17. Quoted in Szulc, *Fidel,* pp. 112–13.

18. Quoted in Shnookal and Tabío, *Fidel,* p. 3.

Chapter 2: Student, Lawyer, and Rebel

19. Quoted in Osvaldo Salas and Roberto Salas, *Fidel's Cuba: A Revolution in Pictures.* New York: Thunder's Mouth Press, 1998, p. 32.

20. Quoted in Betto, *Fidel and Religion,* p. 149.

21. Szulc, *Fidel,* p. 137.

22. Clive Foss, *Fidel Castro.* Stroud, England: Sutton Publishing, 2000, p. 15.

23. Quoted in Shnookal and Tabío, *Fidel,* p. 112.

24. Foss, *Fidel Castro,* pp. 18–19.

25. Quoted in Geyer, *Guerrilla Prince,* p. 84.

26. Foss, *Fidel Castro,* pp. 21–22.

27. Quoted in Lockwood, *Castro's Cuba, Cuba's Fidel,* p. 141.

28. Quoted in Quirk, *Fidel Castro,* p. 55.

29. Quoted in Hugh Thomas, *Cuba, or, The Pursuit of Freedom.* New York: Da Capo Press, 1998, p. 851.

30. Quoted in Jeffrey M. Elliot and Mervyn M. Dymally, *Fidel Castro: Nothing Can Stop the Course of History.* New York: Pathfinder Press, 1986, p. 230.

31. Quoted in Quirk, *Fidel Castro,* p. 69.

32. Quoted in Quirk, *Fidel Castro,* p. 57.

33. Quoted in Szulc, *Fidel,* p. 316.

34. Quoted in Geyer, *Guerrilla Prince,* pp. 119–20.

35. Quoted in Szulc, *Fidel,* p. 324.

36. Quoted in Salas and Salas, *Fidel's Cuba,* p. 33.

37. Quoted in Lockwood, *Castro's Cuba, Cuba's Fidel,* p. 143.

38. Foss, *Fidel Castro,* p. 36.

Chapter 3: The Revolutionary Triumphs

39. Quoted in Elliot and Dymally, *Fidel Castro,* p. 25.

40. Quoted in Szulc, *Fidel*, p. 29.

41. Quirk, *Fidel Castro*, p. 128.

42. Quoted in Szulc, *Fidel*, p. 387.

43. Quoted in Lockwood, *Castro's Cuba, Cuba's Fidel*, p. 169.

44. Quoted in Salas and Salas, *Fidel's Cuba*, p. 10.

45. Quoted in Lockwood, *Castro's Cuba, Cuba's Fidel*, p. 145.

46. Quoted in Elliot and Dymally, *Fidel Castro*, p. 229.

47. Quoted in Quirk, *Fidel Castro*, p. 196.

48. Quirk, *Fidel Castro*, p. 130.

49. Quoted in Foss, *Fidel Castro*, p. 39.

50. Quoted in Quirk, *Fidel Castro*, p. 132.

51. Quirk, *Fidel Castro*, p. 134.

52. Quoted in Salas and Salas, *Fidel's Cuba*, p. 75.

53. Quoted in Geyer, *Guerrilla Prince*, p. 166.

54. Quirk, *Fidel Castro*, p. 175.

55. Quoted in Szulc, *Fidel*, p. 51.

56. Szulc, *Fidel*, p. 445.

57. Szulc, *Fidel*, p. 459.

58. Quirk, *Fidel Castro*, p. 214.

59. Quoted in Salas and Salas, *Fidel's Cuba*, p. 47.

60. Lockwood, *Castro's Cuba, Cuba's Fidel*, p. 7.

61. Quoted in Quirk, *Fidel Castro*, p. 238.

62. Quoted in Geyer, *Guerrilla Prince*, p. 226.

Chapter 4: El Líder Máximo

63. Quoted in Quirk, *Fidel Castro*, p. 231.

64. Quoted in Elliot and Dymally, *Fidel Castro*, pp. 35–36.

65. Quoted in Quirk, *Fidel Castro*, p. 255.

66. Quirk, *Fidel Castro*, p. 262.

67. Quoted in Lockwood, *Castro's Cuba, Cuba's Fidel*, p. 84.

68. Foss, *Fidel Castro*, p. 62.

69. Geyer, *Guerrilla Prince*, p. 256.

70. Quoted in Szulc, *Fidel*, p. 519.

71. Quoted in Thomas, *Cuba, or, The Pursuit of Freedom*, p. 1,489.

72. Quoted in Quirk, *Fidel Castro*, p. 320.

73. Quoted in Geyer, *Guerrilla Prince*, p. 264.

74. Quoted in Szulc, *Fidel*, p. 555.

75. Quoted in Quirk, *Fidel Castro*, p. 438.

76. Thomas, *Cuba, or, The Pursuit of Freedom*, p. 1,419.

77. Quoted in Foss, *Fidel Castro*, p. 71.

78. Quoted in Szulc, *Fidel*, p. 493.

79. Quoted in Elliot and Dymally, *Fidel Castro*, p. 219.

80. Juan O. Tomayo, "Castro's Family: Fidel's Private Life with His Wife and Sons Is So Secret That Even the CIA Is Left to Wonder," *Miami Herald*, October 8, 2000.

81. Foss, *Fidel Castro*, p. 74.

82. Quoted in Betto, *Fidel and Religion*, p. 50.

83. Quoted in Szulc, *Fidel*, pp. 80–81.

84. Quoted in Salas and Salas, *Fidel's Cuba*, p. 94.

85. Quoted in Lockwood, *Castro's Cuba, Cuba's Fidel*, p. 179.

86. Quoted in Salas and Salas, *Fidel's Cuba*, p. 101.

Chapter 5: The Firebrand at Home and Abroad

87. Quoted in Thomas, *Cuba, or, The Pursuit of Freedom*, p. 1,438.

88. Geyer, *Guerrilla Prince*, p. 322.

89. Geyer, *Guerrilla Prince*, p. 317.

90. Szulc, *Fidel*, p. 627.

91. Thomas, *Cuba, or, The Pursuit of Freedom*, p. 1,497.

92. Szulc, *Fidel*, pp. 628–29.

93. Quoted in Quirk, *Fidel Castro*, p. 749.

94. Quoted in Geyer, *Guerrilla Prince*, p. 337.

95. Szulc, *Fidel*, p. 640.

96. Quoted in Salas and Salas, *Fidel's Cuba*, p. 55.

97. Geyer, *Guerrilla Prince*, p. 356.

98. Foss, *Fidel Castro*, p. 92.

99. Quoted in Quirk, *Fidel Castro*, p. 804.

100. Quoted in Elliot and Dymally, *Fidel Castro*, p. 75.

Chapter 6: Hard Times

101. Quoted in Quirk, *Fidel Castro*, p. 827.

102. Quoted in Foss, *Fidel Castro*, p. 94.

103. Foss, *Fidel Castro*, p. 105.

104. Quoted in Quirk, *Fidel Castro*, pp. 829–30.

105. Quoted in Quirk, *Fidel Castro*, p. 831.

106. Geyer, *Guerrilla Prince*, p. 404.

107. Quoted in Thomas, *Cuba, or, The Pursuit of Freedom*, p. 1,481.

108. Geyer, *Guerrilla Prince*, p. 387.

109. Foss, *Fidel Castro*, p. 106.

Epilogue: Holding On

110. Quoted in Elliot and Dymally, *Fidel Castro*, pp. 216–17.

111. Quoted in Elliot and Dymally, *Fidel Castro*, p. 209.

112. Quoted in Elliot and Dymally, *Fidel Castro*, p. 228.

113. Quoted in Tomayo, "Castro's Family."

114. Foss, *Fidel Castro*, p. xiii.

115. Geyer, *Guerrilla Prince*, p. 409.

For Further Reading

Judith Bentley, *Fidel Castro of Cuba.* Englewood Cliffs, NJ: Julian Messner, 1991. A well-written biography, though low on direct quotes and without footnotes.

Warren Brown, *Fidel Castro: Cuban Revolutionary.* Brookfield, CT: Millbrook Press, 1994. This is a good biography for young adults.

Petra Press, *Fidel Castro.* Chicago, IL: Heinemann Library, 2000. A brief, well-illustrated book for younger readers.

John J. Vail, *Fidel Castro.* New York: Chelsea House, 1988. This biography for young adults is well written and illustrated.

Works Consulted

Books

Frei Betto, ed., *Fidel and Religion: Castro Talks on Revolution and Religion with Frei Betto.* New York: Simon and Schuster, 1987. Despite the title, these conversations with a Brazilian priest range over many topics.

Jeffrey M. Elliot and Mervyn M. Dymally, *Fidel Castro: Nothing Can Stop the Course of History.* New York: Pathfinder Press, 1986. This is an extensive interview with Castro, by Elliot, a professor of political science, and Dymally, then a U.S. representative from California.

Clive Foss, *Fidel Castro.* Stroud, England: Sutton Publishing, 2000. Part of a series entitled "Sutton Pocket Biographies," this clearly written and concise book is by a professor of history at the University of Massachusetts.

Georgie Anne Geyer, *Guerrilla Prince: The Untold Story of Fidel Castro.* Kansas City, MO: Andrews and McMeel, 2001. A thorough but unsympathetic book by a longtime overseas correspondent.

Lee Lockwood, *Castro's Cuba, Cuba's Fidel.* New York: Macmillan, 1967. This extensive interview with Castro was conducted in 1965 by a veteran photojournalist.

Robert E. Quirk, *Fidel Castro.* New York: Norton, 1993. A massive, rather dry book by a historian of Latin America that is considered the definitive biography.

Osvaldo Salas and Roberto Salas, *Fidel's Cuba: A Revolution in Pictures.* New York: Thunder's Mouth Press, 1998. This fascinating book is by a father-and-son pair of photographers who document Castro and his land, with comments by Roberto Salas and others.

Deborah Shnookal and Pedro Álvarez Tabío, eds., *Fidel: My Early Years.* Melbourne, Australia: Ocean Press, 1998. This is a collection of the young Castro's autobiographical writings.

Tad Szulc, *Fidel: A Critical Portrait.* New York: Morrow, 1986. A dated but useful biography by a veteran reporter. Despite the title, it is surprisingly sympathetic.

Hugh Thomas, *Cuba, or, The Pursuit of Freedom.* New York: Da Capo Press, 1998. An updated edition of a distinguished historian's classic study, originally published in 1971.

Periodicals

Isabel Garcia-Zarza, "Neighborhood Watch Turns 40," *Sun-Sentinel,* October 20, 2000.

Wayne S. Smith, "Fidel Castro Is No Osama bin Laden," *Los Angeles Times,* June 16, 2002.

Juan O. Tomayo, "Castro's Family: Fidel's Private Life with His Wife and Sons Is So Secret That Even the CIA Is Left to Wonder," *Miami Herald,* October 8, 2000.

Index

Picture Credits

About the Author

Adam Woog is the author of over thirty books for adults, young adults, and children. He has a special interest in biography and history. He lives with his wife and daughter in his hometown of Seattle, Washington.